BUSINESS THE SONY WAY

SECRETS of the World's Most Innovative Electronics Giant

SHU SHIN LUH

CAPSTONE

Copyright © John Wiley & Sons (Asia) Pte Ltd

First published 2003 by
John Wiley & Sons (Asia) for
Capstone Publishing Limited (A Wiley Company)
8 Newtec Place
Magdalen Road
Oxford OX4 1RE
United Kingdom
http://www.capstoneideas.com

CIP catalogue records for this book are available from the British Library
and the US Library of Congress

Typeset in 11/15 pt New Baskerville by Linographic Services Pte Ltd
Printed in Singapore by Saik Wah Press Pte Ltd.
10 9 8 7 6 5 4 3 2 1

CONTENTS

ACKNOWLEDGMENTS

This book would not have been possible without the leap of faith Nick Wallwork, Janis Soo and John Wiley and Sons took in me. I am tremendously grateful to Nick in particular for giving me this valuable opportunity. It has truly been a challenging but rewarding learning experience.

Although Sony did not grant me interviews with its executives, its staff in its Corporate Communications Department met with me numerous times in Tokyo, Los Angeles and New York to respond to my requests promptly. My heartfelt thanks to them for the information and the candidness with which they answered my questions. In particular I wish to thank Gerald Cavanagh for helping me arrange meetings with his colleagues in the U.S. and Japan, and for patiently accommodating my often troublesome requests; Jyunji Tsuyuki and Eiichi Yamamoto for sharing detailed accounts of the VAIO computer's development. Individual Sony employees and consultants who have worked with Sony over the years were also helpful and open when approached about the company's business strategies and corporate culture. To those who willingly helped me with my research and shared their personal Sony experiences, I am extremely grateful.

In writing this book, I owe thanks to many who tirelessly read through drafts of many of the chapters. Thanks to Kirsten Scharnberg, Stacy Atlas and Elizabeth Hughes for teaching me the craft of writing. Thanks to Janet Chung and Marcus Lopez for offering me practical insights on the intricacies of the business world. A special thanks to Tien-Yau Luh and Shou-Jen Hu, both of whom kept pushing me to stay focused and move forward; and to John Owen, for helping me find better ways to tell the story. And most importantly, I am indebted to Chen May Yee and Ilan Greenberg, both of whom tirelessly combed through my drafts over and over again, always with dedication and relentless enthusiasm in the face of a tight timetable.

This book is dedicated to all, named and unnamed, who have helped make this book possible. You know who you are.

Shu Shih Luh
Taipei, Taiwan

PREFACE

At night, the sign "Sony" shines blue and bright over the two-story tiled-roof Japanese houses in the Gotenyama neighborhood on the southern edge of Tokyo, the stomping grounds of the world's most reputable consumer-electronics company and the birthplace of some of the world's most popular electronics goods.

Just take a look around your living room. Do you have a Trinitron television? Or a Walkman? Or perhaps a VAIO computer? Do you own DVDs of *Charlie's Angels*? Or *Men In Black*? Or *Jerry McGuire*? What about CDs by artists like Macy Gray or Yo Yo Ma or Aerosmith or Billie Holiday?

If you answered "Yes" to any of the above, you own a part of the Sony family. And soon, if Sony gets its way, you will be downloading Sony Pictures movie trailers onto your Sony mobile phone, transferring them to your Sony Trinitron television or emailing them to your friends through your Sony VAIO computer. At Sony's annual strategy meeting in May 2002, current chairman Nobuyuki Idei sketched out a vision for this new Sony — one that would transform Sony from simply a maker of cutting-edge, high-quality, stand-alone gadgets into a broadband entertainment giant that would embrace the arrival of the Internet and digitization. The key to this transformation is connectivity, meaning that anything Sony produces will be able to link with any other, anywhere, any time. Sony wants its products to become so ubiquitous in our lives that we don't even notice anymore. At that point, Sony becomes a way of life.

This book aims to tell the story of Sony Corporation's past and present as a way to shed light on the company's future. It serves both as a narrative history of a company that has given the world Walkmans and Trinitron color televisions, and as a case study for how entrepreneurs, with the right combination of tenacity, passion, creativity and an eye for the future, can build a company from the humblest of beginnings into a global giant, with operating revenues of more than US$50 billion and more than 168,000 employees. Sony has played a key role in the evolution of electronics in the last half-century, from our reliance on radios to black-and-white televisions to crisply colored flat-screen televisions. But it has also developed beyond the traditional realms of a consumer-electronics company to become a maker of movies, music and video games.

The book provides an insight into the vision and drive of the corporation's founders, Masaru Ibuka and Akio Morita, that led the company's transformation from a small radio-repair shop in a bombed-out department store in central Tokyo into today's diversified giant. Ibuka and Morita built their company around two core values: teamwork and innovation. These values are as evident today as they were at the outset. Ibuka held innovation above all things, even profitability and fame, and wanted to build a company that would provide engineers with an environment in which they could invent and take risks to their hearts' content. The company, in essence, would be a second family to all.

It is hard now to imagine the conditions in which Ibuka and Morita had to operate little more than half a century ago. As Morita wrote in his 1985 autobiography, *Made in Japan*: "The evidence of defeat [from the Second World War] was all around us. We could see bomb damage wherever we looked. There were leaks in the roof and we literally had to open umbrellas over our desks sometimes...In order to get to the rooms where Tokyo Tsushin Kogyo [Sony's original name] was located, you had to duck under some clotheslines on which the neighbors sometimes had their children's diapers drying in the breeze."

Sony's headquarters still sits today in the same neighborhood in which it started out. It was here that Sony, with ¥190,000 seed capital, took its first steps toward becoming a world-renowned consumer-electronics giant. It was here that Sony's first product, a transistor radio, was born. And it is here that Ibuka and Morita created the name that has become synonymous with cutting-edge, high-quality consumer products. The landscape of the neighborhood has changed over the years. Now, Gotenyama is quickly becoming a popular commercial area for businesses squeezed out of the overcrowded parts of central Tokyo. Across the narrow lane from today's Sony headquarters, a bluish-gray glass building that stands eight stories high, is the very plot of land where the first Sony offices stood more than five decades ago. Office buildings have shot up in their place, many housing Sony's research and development teams.

Today, visitors to the opulent Sony headquarters can stop by the company's museum where rows of glass displays showcase Sony's many successes to date. Amongst these is a display for the Tape-corder, which includes a message recorded on the machine by Ibuka in August 1950 to mark the first anniversary of the machine's production.

Across the spacious lobby, visitors can wave hello to Sony's future, the AIBO robots, Macaron and Latte. These bear-like robotic pets are equipped with artificial intelligence that enables them to greet customers and clients with nods and beeping sounds.

Like the visitor caught between the museum and the AIBO robots, Sony itself is standing at the nexus of its past and future. Today, the digitization of the world — both in the way we live and the way we use electronics — has changed the consumer-electronics industry. The rapid changes in technology and the advent of the Broadband Age have made it difficult for Sony to rest on the laurels it earned in the analog era. To counter the formidable competition coming from all directions, Sony has tried to broaden its business internally, adding to its portfolio a mobile-phone joint venture, a movie studio, a record label and a video-game business. It is also beginning to engage the new rules of business, working with companies that used to be sworn rivals. How Sony will fare in this new business era remains to be determined. But if Sony's history of tenacity and innovation is any indication, then it is likely that the company will be able to weather this digital battle and remain a strong competitor in the marketplace.

SONY CORPORATION IN BRIEF

Global Headquarters: Tokyo

Founding Date: May 7, 1946

Founders: Masaru Ibuka and Akio Morita

Operating Revenue (2002): US$62 billion

Operating Income (2002): US$1.1 billion

Chairman and Chief Executive Officer: Nobuyuki Idei

President and Chief Operating Officer: Kunitake Ando

Major Consolidated Subsidiaries Worldwide: 97

Number of Employees: 168,000

Source: Sony Corporation, Company filings from the U.S. Securities Exchange Commission

Throughout its 50-plus years, Sony has set a lot of firsts for Japanese corporations. It was the first Japanese company to be listed on the New York Stock Exchange. It was the first in the world to utilize transistor technology in the manufacture of transistor radios. It was the first Japanese company to buy an American record label and movie studio. In the process, Sony dispelled the stereotypical image associated with the

"Made in Japan" label and let the world know that Japanese goods were more than cheap trinkets. It has shown the world the might of Japanese corporations. But it has also had to face the dilemma of juggling its Japanese traditions with Westernized management philosophies. Now, it finds itself challenged to establish a new place in today's digital business era.

The increasing numbers of standard technologies available on the marketplace have helped level the playing field and allowed Sony's rivals to quickly bring products to market. The company can no longer depend solely on its technological capabilities for its competitive edge. There are many — analysts, competitors, industry observers — who wonder whether Sony will be able to reinvent and refine itself quickly enough to keep pace with the realities and changing rules of our business environment today and in the future. But just as the Sony of 50 years ago was a different kind of company from the Sony of today, there is little doubt that the company will evolve in the next 50 years, responding to changes in the business climate and setting new precedents along the way. What Sony executives and observers are convinced will remain the same is the constant drive to think outside conventional wisdom and capture the imagination of the consumers around the world. Sony will always strive to produce the high-quality products and services — whether in electronics or entertainment — that will, it believes, continue to make consumers around the world exclaim, "Ah, it's a Sony!"

MAJOR MILESTONES IN SONY HISTORY

May 1946
- Tokyo Tsushin Kogyo (Tokyo Telecommunications Engineering Corporation), also known as Totsuko, established in Nihonbashi, Tokyo

July 1950
- Japan's first magnetic tape recorder, the G-Type, launched

August 1955
- Japan's first transistor radio, the TR-55, launched

December 1957
- Sony's first overseas transistor radio, the TR-63, launched in the U.S.

January 1958
- Company name changed to Sony Corporation

December 1958
- Sony listed on the Tokyo Stock Exchange

February 1960
- Sony Corporation of America established

December 1960
- World's first transistor television, the TV8-301, launched

June 1961
- Sony offers shares in form of American Depository Receipts (ADRs) on the over-the-counter market of the New York Stock Exchange

April 1966
- Sony showroom in Ginza, Tokyo, opened

March 1968
- CBS/Sony Records Inc., a 50–50 joint venture with CBS Inc. of the U.S., established (It became a wholly owned Sony subsidiary in January 1988 and was renamed Sony Music Entertainment in April 1991.)

October 1968
- Trinitron color TV, the KV-1310, launched

September 1970
- Sony shares listed on the New York Stock Exchange

September 1972
- Sony hires Harvey Schein to head the company's U.S. operations

May 1975
- Home-use Betamax VCR, the SL-6300, launched

July 1979
- First personal-headphone stereo Walkman, the TPS-L2, launched

August 1982
- Announcement of Sony-Philips compact-disc technology

January 1985
- Debut of Sony's 8mm Handycam Camcorder

January 1988
- Acquires CBS Records Inc. (renamed Sony Music Entertainment Inc in January 1991)

June 1989
- Appointment of first two non-Japanese employees, Michael Schulhof and Jakob Schmuckli, to Board of Directors

November 1989
- Acquires Columbia Pictures Entertainment Inc. (renamed Sony Pictures Entertainment in August 1991)

June 1991
- First outside director appointed to Sony's Board of Directors

January 1993
- Michael Schulhof appointed head of U.S. operations

November 1993
- Sony Computer Entertainment Inc., home of the Sony PlayStation®, established

December 1993
- PlayStation console officially launched in Japan

November 1994
- Sony stuns Wall Street and Hollywood by announcing losses at Sony Pictures Entertainment, the first time it admits to financial troubles at the studio

April 1995
- Nobuyuki Idei becomes president of Sony (He becomes chairman in June, 2000 and remains chairman and chief executive officer.)

July 1997
- VAIO desktop computer makes its debut.

August 1997
- Sir Howard Stringer joins Sony Corporation of America as president

December 1997
- Death of Masaru Ibuka

October 1999
- Death of Akio Morita

August 2000
- Clié handheld organizer introduced in Japan

Source: Genryu, Sony Corporation

One

ANCHORING THE SHOP: WEAVING THE FAMILIAL WEB

How Sony rose from the tiny radio-repair shop in a bomb-ravaged Tokyo after the Second World War to a $50-billion, globe-straddling giant has a lot to do with the relationship between brilliant engineer Masuru Ibuka and his apprentice/co-founder, Akio Morita. Their friendship, and that of the family members and professional managers they groomed, highlights the trust and faith that contributed to Sony's triumphs and setbacks.

In the 1980s when Akio Morita, co-founder of Sony, was chairman and already a Japanese business icon, he would give an annual welcome speech to new recruits that strikingly sums up the Sony corporate culture. In essence, what he said to them was this: I want everyone to feel happy being at Sony. It is a challenge to Sony to pay you salary without knowing what your potential contributions might be. So I ask you to start learning quickly and to contribute to Sony as soon as possible. But if you ever start to wonder whether you should work here, please quit and look for another job. We want people who want to be with us.

For Morita, his co-founder Masaru Ibuka, and the executives they nurtured, the company represented more than just a group of salarymen who happened to get up every morning to come to work at the same company. For them, Sony equaled family, and every member of the company should be treated like they were part of the family. It is this belief in the corporation as a family that lifted Sony from the tiny radio-repair shop in a bomb-ravaged Tokyo after the Second World War to a $50-billion, globe-straddling consumer-electronics giant.

Between Ibuka and Morita was a friendship and trust that resembled brotherly love. Ibuka was the thinker of the Sony family; Morita was the executer. Employees found their two-step arrangement flawless and the founders' conviction percolated through the company. The result: relationships between employees and employer akin to a second family.

This belief in the company as family underscores a widespread management style in Asia that puts teamwork and loyalty above pure profits and cost-benefit analysis. From this family foundation derives a composite of Sony that is neither wholly Japanese nor entirely Western; rather, it is a hybrid of corporate management styles that has contributed to Sony's triumphs and setbacks.

"The company equals family" formula is one found all over Asia, in corporate worlds that are dominated largely by family-run businesses and regional conglomerates where everyone knows everyone, and business deals are sometimes sealed with a handshake at the dinner table. The attitude centers on a belief that employees feel a distinct sense of familial obligation to the corporation and not simply because they get paid to be there. Leaders of prominent Japanese companies speak often of entry into a company as like being born again into another family. Sony executives are no exception. In return, just as parents guarantee a lifetime of undying love and support, the company offers them a lifetime guarantee of job security and a promise of healthy compensation.

Critics believe this management style is not sufficiently transparent and could lead to a lack of accountability and a stagnant workforce. There are numerous examples of companies that have become too nepotistic, neglecting fundamental priorities of the business; that is, to generate a revenue stream. During the Asian financial crisis in the late 1990s, some analysts blamed the demise of many Asian businesses on the tendency for family ties to blur the distinction between business and personal relationships, and for confusing family loyalty with professionalism and accountability. But while criticism of some of these intricate corporate webs was justified, these tight-knit internal networks have produced fierce loyalty within the company, undoubtedly one of the crucial ingredients for a successful Asian company.

In the West there is considerably more fluidity when it comes to corporate executives hopping from one company to another every few years. In such circumstances it is harder to build a company based entirely on a stable web of personal relationships, trust and loyalty. For one, there simply is not time to nurture the trust and leverage the strengths of each executive in top management with so much mobility. While Asian companies are becoming more Westernized, paying a premium for management consultancies to tell them how to structure their companies and formulate their business strategies, many corporations continue to hold one traditional business principle dear — loyalty. In return for their employees' loyalty, they offer lifetime employment.

WEAVING A FAMILY WEB

Given Sony's history, it is not difficult to understand why Sony holds on tightly to this idea of family, even today when the model of corporate loyalty and lifetime obligation is beginning to wane, even in Asia. Most of Sony's top executives have worked for the company for more than two decades. Akira Higuchi, one of the original seven engineers who followed Ibuka to Tokyo in October 1945 to found the company that would become Sony, still carries a title "adviser". He drives himself to work by 8 a.m. and spends his day receiving visitors and organizing his papers.[1]

FOSTERING LOYALTY

Like parents who guarantee a lifetime of undying love and support, by offering employees a lifetime of job security and healthy compensation, the corporation receives in return unwavering loyalty and dedication from employees.

This requires treating employees as equals, giving them room to take risks, speak up, and rewarding them with promotions and better compensation for their accomplishments.

Perhaps some would argue that the concept of family developed out of necessity. The original group of Sony engineers were drawn together immediately following Japan's defeat in 1945. Instead of joining established family conglomerates with an unending supply of capital and political clout, these engineers wanted a fresh start — a company in which they could invest their knowledge, skills and dreams. So, these seven engineers followed Ibuka to a bombed-out department store in the center of Tokyo. Ibuka, the leader of this group of hopeful engineers, recognized that he would need to get government backing and a hefty capital base if they were to realize their collective and individual dreams.[2]

Call Sony fortunate if you will. Through friends and introductions from friends to potential investors, Sony engineers secured the ¥190,000 seed money to test out their imagination. Ibuka and Morita, coming from well-established families connected to business and politics, were able to find a board of advisers who had real stature to back a fledgling company. Through these connections, Morita and Ibuka received introductions that they could not possibly have arranged on their own. Sony's early advisers/benefactors included Ibuka's father-in-law, Tamon Maeda, a former Minister of Education; Michiji Tajima, Maeda's university friend and an influential financier; Rin Matsutani, the man who gave Ibuka his first big job, at Photo-chemical Laboratories; and Morita's father, Kyuzaemon Morita.[3]

Sony's founding fathers, were also lucky to find a group of like-minded engineers willing to work together as a team (with few of the class divisions that marked the traditional Japanese corporate hierarchy) through failures that almost bankrupted the firm many times over and successes that almost persuaded them to stop pursuing bigger dreams. It is the gumption of these early engineers, their trust in one another, and their drive to challenge others and each other that have built Sony into a global brand. In the true fashion of a family unit, almost all of the original team of engineers stayed with Sony until they retired.

LIFETIME EMPLOYMENT

The concept of an employee spending all of his working life with a single company is not necessarily a solely Japanese invention, but it is certainly one that the Japanese companies have perpetuated.

The concept of lifetime employment works as follows: in linking his future with that of the company, an individual is taking considerable risk — regardless of how long he plans to stay with the company. What happens to the company during his time there clearly has an impact on his career. Because of this risk, which the individual willingly takes for the company, and to reward him for his loyalty, the company undertakes to care for the recruit for his entire career.

As a result, pay and promotion in most Japanese companies is largely determined by length of service. There are, of course, exceptions to the rule, where young, energetic, promising workers leapfrog over more senior people on the corporate ladder. Sony itself presents a clear example of this with its appointment of Nobuyuki Idei as president. Idei is a Sony lifer who started in 1960, straight out of Tokyo's prestigious Waseda University. But when he was offered the top job in April 1995, he basically leapfrogged a dozen more senior executives with nicknames like "Mr. Walkman", "Mr. Semiconductor", and "Mr. Camcorder", for their roles in Sony's engineering triumphs.

There is a definite trade-off for the die-hard loyalty found in Japanese companies. Most significantly, this restricts flexibility in personnel management and has three main drawbacks:[4]

- The Japanese workforce cannot quickly adjust to downturns. A company has to depend first on reduction of temporary work; then, on pulling subcontracted work back within the company; then, on offering special retirement allowances to encourage workers to withdraw from the workforce; and, finally, allowing attrition to do its work. Only in acute crisis, only after exhausting other approaches, and only with the full agreement of the union and workforce, do actual layoffs or dismissals take place.
- A company also runs the risk of having a bloated payroll, retaining staff who may be less than competent. Critics argue that, because performance reviews play no part in determining whether or not people keep their jobs, lifetime employment can act as a disincentive to workers. As a result, the company may be stuck with unenthusiastic staff that may be redundant but can't be laid off, creating a financial burden and slowing the company's growth.

- Lifetime employment also makes it extremely difficult to bring about acquisitions or mergers. The fastest way for a company to grow and enter a new business area is often through acquisitions. Although mergers and acquisitions certainly have their own risks, these may not be as great sometimes as growing organically, through internal diversification. Internal growth may pose a greater threat to the company's overall financial stability and is considerably more time-consuming.

Having said all this, lifetime employment is no longer an entrenched management philosophy in Japan today. Economic recession has worn down the financial capabilities of even the largest conglomerates. Even Sony has been forced to rethink its personnel policies. When Nobuyuki Idei became chairman, he instituted a restructuring plan that has reduced the board of directors from 38 to 10 and promises to shrink the workforce at the company's headquarters from the present 2,500 to a few hundred within the next five years, and introduce a global downsizing of 10 per cent.

For some people, the term "lifetime employment" conjures negative impressions such as sluggishness, staleness and, most seriously, sacrificing independence and individuality. But, in Japan, they have a nicer phrase for it: *nihonteki keiei* or "Japanese-style management". As Sony's track record proves, lifetime employment has hardly translated into lackluster business strategies. Here at Sony, loyalty and this true sense of familial belonging have woven together a web of creative, intelligent and passionate individuals with trust that guarantees minimum staff turnover and a wealth of institutional knowledge of Sony's work and innovative corporate culture.

Norio Ohga provides one of the best examples of this. Unlike many of the early Sony men born of engineering backgrounds, Ohga, Sony's third chairman (1995–1999), was a music student, on his way to becoming an opera singer when Morita discovered him. Ohga had written critical letters to Sony, pointing out the flaws of the company's first tape recorder, the G-Type Tape-corder. Ohga pointed out that the playback was too distorted to be of any use to a musician. Using the metaphor of a dancer's reliance on the mirror to help her improve her posture and see her flaws, Ohga argued that the Tape-corder should play a similar role for singers and musicians. His criticisms of the tape recorder, which was Sony's pride, and his keen observations and honesty impressed Morita, who offered to pay Ohga a full starting salary in return for his thoughts on the future of recording technology. But Ohga was determined to be an opera singer and refused Morita's offer, saying that he had no intention of becoming a businessman.

> "They actually treated me as an equal, and that was an attitude you would never have found in any normal Japanese business executive."
> — Norio Ohga, Sony chairman (1995–1999)

Undeterred, Morita proposed to let Ohga advise the company on various products, with no full-time commitments necessary, while pursuing his singing career. Ohga agreed and, before long, had become a familiar figure at Sony. He was invited to attend technical meetings, impressing everyone with his encyclopedic knowledge of tape recorders in particular. Over the years, while Ohga pursued his opera career, Morita kept in close touch through weekly letters, sending him models of Sony's products to comment on, while courting him to join the company full-time. But it would be another six years before Morita succeeded.

Ohga finally made the leap to Sony one night when he realized that his double life was no longer sustainable. He was singing the role of Count Almaviva in *The Marriage of Figaro* and had arrived at the theater in Hiroshima at the end of an exhausting day spent in a futile attempt to sell Sony tape recorders to a local affiliate. With just enough time to get into costume and makeup, Ohga went on stage and sang his way without incident through the first three acts. With the demanding portion of the performance behind him, Ohga changed costume and sat down on a trunk backstage to wait for the count's final entrance at the end of Act Four. Exhausted, he dozed off, only awaking when the orchestra played the cue for his entrance. He realized in a panic that he was sitting on the wrong side of the stage. With no choice, he appeared on stage from an unexpected direction and threw Figaro and Susanna off their timing. That night, he resolved to give up his musical career.

Years later, he said in an interview that he chose business over music because he felt a sense of responsibility to the people working for him at Sony. By that time, as head of the entire tape recorder division, Ohga had a staff of more than 1,000 employees. The opera incident aside, what ultimately convinced Ohga that he had to work for Sony was the co-founders' warmth and respect for the people who worked for them. "They actually treated me as an equal, and that was an attitude you would never have found in any normal

Japanese business executive," he said, recalling his early involvement with Sony.

On joining the Sony family, Ohga dedicated himself to the company. In return, Morita and Ibuka demonstrated their unique management style of nurturing and fast-tracking talent, and moved him quickly up through the ranks. Within two years, in addition to managing the tape recorder division, Ohga also oversaw product planning, industrial design and advertising for the whole company. In 1995, as Morita's protégé, he ascended to the chairmanship of Sony.

It is important here to step back and point out that although lifetime loyalty and obligation to the company inspire stereotypes about bored employees, at Sony, where creativity had always been a brand trademark, the company strove not to allow innovation to suffer because of the company's emphasis on the idea of family values. In fact, creativity flourishes because of the kind of balance Sony is able to strike between respect for individuality and need for teamwork. In many ways, by striking this balance, Sony defies the rigid framework of traditional Japanese corporations. Its willingness to take risks and experiment, and its knack for bold marketing and branding, are digressions from the typical conservative, hierarchical Japanese corporate world.

To truly understand how Sony maintains this balance, it is necessary to first understand and appreciate the innovative approach taken from the outset by Ibuka, Morita and their team of engineers. Through mutual trust and a shared belief in this new family, they built a foundation upon which they could share their common dream of making the tiny company something big.

EXCERPT FROM SONY'S FOUNDING PROSPECTUS

"The road of a pioneer is full of difficulties, but in spite of the many hardships, people of Sony always unite harmoniously and closely because of their joy of participating in creative work and their pride in contributing their own unique talents to this aim. Sony has a principle of respecting and encouraging one's ability — the right man in the right post — and always tries to bring out the best in a person and believes in him and constantly allows him to develop his ability. This is the vital force of Sony."

THE SONY FOUNDERS

The tiny radio-repair shop, Tokyo Telecommunications Engineering Corporation (Tokyo Tsushin Kogyo or Totsuko for short), that was to become the Sony Corporation, emerged from the shadows of the Second World War. In a rare nationwide radio broadcast, Emperor Hirohito had just stunned his nation by admitting defeat, the upheaval from which, together with the reforms that accompanied the U.S. occupation, brought vast changes to the Japanese business landscape.

For decades, family conglomerates such as Matsushita Electric Corp., Mitsubishi Corp. and Toshiba Corp. had controlled the Japanese business community. Post-war Japan no longer belonged solely to the established business leaders and bureaucrats. In the changing business climate, the establishment was losing an advantage over emerging entrepreneurs who had a clear vision of where Japan, and they, might go.

"Everyone is taught
to act like a family
member ready to do
what is necessary."
— Akio Morita,
founder

At 38, Ibuka was 14 years older than Morita and an experienced businessman. During the war, he had built up a substantial business manufacturing measuring and testing devices for the military. With Japan's defeat, Ibuka's business evaporated. Like many others, he gravitated to the radio parts and repair business, a lucrative line of business because of all the American soldiers stationed in Japan who brought with them their electronic gadgets.

Morita's business experience differed markedly from that of Ibuka. He was the heir to a commercial empire that included a sake brewery, a soy sauce and miso enterprise, and one of Japan's largest flour and bread companies. He grew up with chauffeur-driven cars, servants and every Western convenience at his disposal. By the time he was 24 years old in 1948, Morita had been attending business meetings with his father for more than a decade.[5]

But Morita's great passion in life was not sake but electronics. This was where he and Ibuka, his mentor and wartime buddy, found common ground. A gifted electrical engineering student at Osaka Imperial University, Morita was recruited in the middle of the war into the navy, which was an important training ground for Japan's post-war generation of electrical engineers. Here, Morita worked on heat-seeking guidance systems. During this research, he met Ibuka, who was working on a system to detect submarines.

After the war, Morita could have opted for a plush life as head of an established family business. Instead, he joined Ibuka to start a small company with an uncertain future. In this sense, he showed the kind of entrepreneurship and opportunism that would become a hallmark of the new post-war order, and build the foundation for their future company.

Like so many successful post-war enterprises in Japan, Totsuko mixed deep links to the pre-war and wartime establishment with a measure of flesh blood. Ibuka's father-in-law, Maeda Tamon, and Morita's wealthy father threw their support and political influence behind the Sony founders. These heavy hitters brought on board powerful supporters, such as the legendary Bandai Junichiro, former head of the great Mitsui Bank — a vital contact when it came to arranging all-important financing.

With such support and a cohort of enthusiastic former military engineers, Ibuka and Morita laid the foundation for their Sony family. Over the years, a potent mix of Morita's charisma and Ibuka's enthusiasm was directly responsible for attracting and keeping a range of hugely talented people to manage their various businesses.

THE SONY FAMILY

At the base of Sony's family structure are three core values: trust, individuality and creativity. From day one at Sony, these qualities were emphasized to every Sony employee and have governed the way the company interacts with its employees, from the top brass to the workers on the factory floor.

These qualities manifest themselves in the following principles:

MISTAKES ARE OKAY

Western managers pioneered the concept of accountability in the workplace, a way to measure an individual worker's performance and productivity to determine promotions, salaries, demotions, etc. At Sony, questions such as "How did you do on the project?" and "Did the research result in a new product?" play an important role in judging an employee's performance. They are important because they speak to the desire for constant innovation that is at the very core of Sony's corporate spirit. But by the same token, the Sony founders believed in encouraging their employees to be independent and take measured risks. In a pioneering environment, risks must be taken, and, along the way, mistakes will be made. At many companies, mistakes often result in punitive action — demotions, pay cuts or firings. At Sony, however, executives find it unwise and unnecessary to define individual responsibility too clearly. "Everyone is taught to act like a family member ready to do what is necessary," Morita wrote in his 1985 autobiography, *Made In Japan*. "The important thing, in my view is not to pin the blame for a mistake on somebody, but rather to find out what caused the mistake."

In Japan, the idea of collectivism often prevails over individual identity. The corporate family environment creates a nurturing and secure environment where workers are self-motivated and more fearless in their efforts to discover new ways of improving products and innovating. Managers, knowing that the company's ordinary business is carried out by energetic and enthusiastic younger employees, can devote their time and effort to planning the future of the company.

THE ABANDONED ELECTRIC RICE-COOKER

Courtesy of Sony Corporation

The very first product on which Ibuka tried to put the Sony name was an electric rice-cooker, and it was an utter failure. It was 1946, and Sony was struggling to stay alive as a new company as it searched for a product that met Ibuka's high expectations. In the beginning, any means of making honest money had to be considered seriously. Suggestions ranged from selling sweetened miso soup to building a miniature golf course on a burned-out tenement lot.

As war plants closed down, Japan suddenly had more electricity than it could use at the time. This surplus fed Ibuka's desire to produce items that were needed for everyday life. Since rice was a staple in the Japanese diet, he set out to make an electric rice-cooker meant to help housewives with their cooking. The rice-cooker, made by interlocking aluminum electrodes that were connected to the bottom of a wooden tub, was a primitive product. Its effectiveness was dependent on the kind of rice used and the weight of the water, and the results were mostly either undercooked or overcooked. No matter how many times the Sony team tried, the rice just wouldn't come out right.

In the end, they gave up.

Let's look at some examples of Sony's past failures. All of them play a role in shaping the way the company is today:

- **The transistor mistake that almost bankrupted Sony**

In the spring of 1957, Sony was carrying out detailed tests of its manufacturing process to mass-produce the transistor radios that won them international fame. The tests identified the main problem as a misuse of a chemical, antimony, that was quick to erode. Technical director Kazuo Iwama found that phosphorus was a much more effective alternative.

Excited by this discovery, Iwama confidently switched the entire production line over to using phosphorus without doing further testing. In the process, he almost ruined the company. His initial testing was woefully insufficient; thousands of transistors were manufactured under the new method, but not a single one of them worked. Sony had to stop shipping radios altogether.

The problem lay in the ratio of phosphorus to tin, another chemical that had to be added to ensure the stability of the chemical compounds. Only after several months of further study, during which Sony researcher Esaki Leona discovered the effect that would later win him the Nobel Prize, did the team come up with a solution: replacing tin with indium and mixing it 50–50 with the phosphorus. This, finally, was the breakthrough Sony had been looking for. The reject rate fell from 90 per cent to 10 per cent, and Sony's profits soared.

Iwama was not dismissed for making a mistake that almost bankrupted the company. Some have attributed this to the fact that he was married to Morita's younger sister, Kikuko. But other examples involving Ohga or Nobuyuki Idei, who made mistakes that set Sony back in new business developments but later moved on to assume chairmanship of the company, would indicate that Morita believed in his heart that learning from mistakes is more important than simply punishing the perpetrator. Iwama's redemption, so to speak, was figuring out to replace antimony with phosphorus. After finding out that phosphorus alone wouldn't do the trick, Iwama and his research team worked for months to finally come up with the correct formula.

Iwama went on to enjoy a distinguished career at Sony, succeeding Morita as president of the company in 1976. Although a less visible character than Morita outside the organization, he has been venerated inside Sony culture as a cautious, level-headed rationalist who introduced the rigor of scientific method to Sony's research and development process. Iwama's endeavors provide a clear example of the benefits Sony has gained through its policy of allowing employees to learn from their mistakes.

- **The Betamax lesson**

Betamax — Courtesy of Sony Corporation

One of the most heart-breaking failures for Sony, Betamax, was conceived as part of Ibuka's dream to bring multimedia into people's living rooms. He set out with the idea of making the first truly portable video-recording equipment that would enable people to tape their favorite television shows and movies to watch at their leisure. The Betamax was an ingenious innovation, technologically superior to its competitor's version, the Video Home System (VHS), manufactured by JVC (Victor Company of Japan, Ltd.).

But Sony was so preoccupied with refining and tweaking Betamax's technological capabilities, it didn't work hard enough to get companies together in a consortium to support the Betamax format and make it the standard. Sony's rivals in the VHS format did that, and ended up with more companies making that format, even though, technologically, Sony's Betamax produced better sound and visual quality. At the time, one drawback a Japanese executive pointed out about Sony's Betamax was that it couldn't record more than an hour's worth of programming, whereas the VHS machine had longer recording capacity.

Sony had invested a lot of time, money and corporate reputation on the success of Betamax; executives at headquarters had even taken to sporting tiepins and cuff links inscribed with the Betamax logo. For Ibuka and his team, it was mortifying to watch a system that they held to be inferior to their own take the lead in the marketplace — particularly when it had been so closely modeled on their own Betamax. But in typical Sony fashion, Ibuka and his engineers walked away with a clear awareness of where they had gone wrong and were determined not to repeat the same mistake again. Since then, Sony has gone out of its way to get major companies in Japan and overseas to agree on standards for many of its new products such as its 8mm Handycam video recorder, the high-density 3.5-inch floppy disks for minicomputers, and even Sony PlayStation.

- **Cashing out too soon: The calculated mistake**

It was 1964 when Sony started making desktop calculators. Calculators were becoming more commonly used among mass consumers, Sony's target audience. At the time, Sony officials thought it would be a good addition to the product line. At the 1964 New York World Fair, Morita personally went to demonstrate the wonders of Sony's desktop calculator, explaining to visitors Sony's aim to make the world's best, state-of-the-art calculator.

Soon after, Sony started marketing a special calculator model it called the SOBAX, which stood for "solid state abacus". But several dozen other Japanese companies had also jumped into the business of making calculators, and the shakeout would come sooner or later through a very brutal price war. Sony, taking extreme pride in not compromising quality for lower price, did not want to be a part of that battle and thus gave up on its calculator business.

Sure enough, many calculator makers went bankrupt and others got out of the market, taking big losses. Today, there are only three major makers of calculators.

Reflecting on the decision, Morita once said that, in some ways, he felt justified in his decision to pull out of the calculator business. There was still much to be done in audio, television and video to keep Sony engineers challenged and revved up. But he also recognized that he may have been too hasty in this decision. "I confess," he said, "that I think it showed a lack of technical foresight on my part, just the thing I think we have been good at." Had Sony stayed with calculators, Morita believes that the company might have developed early expertise in digital technology, for use later in personal computers and audio and video applications, and could perhaps have given it the jump on its competition. Sony had to acquire this technology later, even though it once had the basis for it right there in house. So from a business viewpoint, while the decision to pull out of manufacturing calculators was correct in the short term, it was one Sony would have to pay for in the long run.

Mistakes happen even to the best and most smoothly run corporations. They happen because of human error, poor judgment, wrong timing, among other reasons. Maybe in the heat of the moment, the significance of a particular failure may seem grave and impossible to overcome. But if a company is able to learn from a mistake and apply those lessons to the future, this can really be seen as an investment rather than a total washout. That is not to say that corporations should allow for reckless mistakes. Morita made a clear distinction between reckless mistakes and learning from mistakes. Branding a person who makes a mistake as a failure and limiting his promotion prospects could result in this worker losing motivation for the rest of his business life and possibly deprive the company of whatever good things he may have to offer later. If, on the other hand, the causes of the mistake are clarified and made public, the person who made the mistake will not forget it, and others will not make the same mistake. "I tell our people, 'Go ahead and do what you think is right. If you make a mistake, you will learn from it. Just don't make the same mistake twice,'" Morita said. The philosophy underscores a Japanese corporate belief that each employee is part of the corporate family for life and that it is more important to try to identify the root cause of the mistake to prevent the problem arising again in the future. Besides, even if the culprit is found, it is likely that he may be a senior employee and the loss of his knowledge and experience will be greater than the cost of finding a replacement. And if it is made clear that the case is being pursued not to cause damage to an individual's future, but to help all employees learn, the result will be a valuable lesson rather than a loss.

TREAT EMPLOYEES LIKE FAMILY

At Sony, the idea of the company as a family surfaces again and again in essays and speeches about corporate culture and management philosophy. It describes a prevalent business culture in Asia. After all, this is a region still dotted with family-owned conglomerates, with ownership passed down through the generations. Family managers surround themselves with professionals who are loyal and dedicated to the company, but these "outsiders" are then considered a part of the family. These relationships go deeper than any financial contract guarantees. In fact, for decades, Sony's top executives worked for Morita and Ibuka without any kind of contract. Even Michael Schulhof, former chairman of Sony Corporation of America and probably the only non-Japanese to be accepted into the innermost circle of Sony's leaders, didn't have a contract until he asked for one in 1993.

The trust that exists between this inner circle and the Sony founders lies in the fundamental value of loyalty: that families don't leave family members behind. Morita alluded to this idea frequently in his autobiography. At Sony, he said, the company and the employee are one. He looked down on massive layoffs during economic downturns, believing that the family should stick together in good and bad times, and that layoffs were a betrayal of workers who sweated and gave their all to shape the company's success. But in recent years, with economic depression in Japan and cyclical ups and downs in the global electronics sector, even Sony has had difficulties adhering to its golden "no layoffs" rule. Between 1999 and 2002, it had to cut the number of manufacturing plants from 70 to 55, and slashed the number of employees from 170,000 to just under 50,000. But industry analysts say that, for the most part, Sony has been less inclined than its competitors to make rash decisions about wide-scale layoffs in bad times. It tries to cut costs by tightening its belt first, using layoffs only as a last resort. For example, in the U.S., Sony Corporation of America instituted a cost-savings plan, known as Project U.S.A., to streamline the company's cost structure. Seeing that its competitors were posting stronger profits, it decided that the American division had to either step up revenue generation or save unnecessary costs. So, under Project U.S.A., Sony restructured the manufacturing and distribution operations in the U.S. to keep inventory and production costs under better control. At Sony Pictures Entertainment, a reduction in profits on the networks has pushed the movie studio to cut back on its television production in the U.S. to save money.

INSTILL LOYALTY

Over the years, few top-brass managers at Sony have been lured away by other companies. This can be partially attributed to the fact that some of the managers were actual family members, related by blood or marriage, or had working with Ibuka or Morita for years. Kazuo Iwama, for example, was Morita's brother-in-law. The Morita and Iwama families were neighbors in Nagoya. A month after Iwama married Morita's younger sister, Kikuko, Morita recruited him to the company. Iwama's accomplishments at Sony are many. He was part of the initial team of engineers who developed the transistor radio in the early 1950s and, until his death from colon cancer in 1982, he remained a loyal employee.

In a highly competitive industry such as consumer electronics, the ability to retain star managers is an impressive feat. When a manager does make the decision to leave Sony, depending on the circumstances, it is largely taken as a tremendous insult. (How can you leave a family? And why would you want to do so?) In its early days, Sony Corporation of America hired a district sales manager whom Morita and others identified as promising. The company flew him to Tokyo on an extended trip to meet everybody at the home office and get acquainted with the philosophy and spirit of Sony. The sales manager did beautifully, impressing everyone in Tokyo. He returned to the U.S. and went on to shine in Sony. But then one day, as Morita recalled it, without any warning, he came into Morita's office and said, "Mr. Morita, thanks for everything, but I'm quitting." A competitor had offered to double or triple his salary and he thought he couldn't refuse it. "I was very embarrassed and embittered by this episode," Morita wrote later. Months later, when he ran into this man at an electronics show, he tried to avoid him and felt awkward when the man rushed over and wanted to introduce him to all the new products he was demonstrating for his new company. But, by the same token, Morita has let brilliant engineers go at times when he felt that he could not offer them the kind of resources and time to develop their own ideas.

The example of Morita fuming over the American manager who left the company illustrates a constant struggle within Sony to balance its core Japanese management philosophy with its quirky Western cultural practices. On the one hand, Sony has thrown off the stodgy and rigid Japanese management tradition. As discussed earlier, its founders wanted to create a corporate environment where creative ideas flowed freely and people — managers and employees — could have candid discussions about new ideas. Walk into Sony Pictures Entertainment in Culver City, California, where major motion pictures are made every day, and the feel of the company and the attitude of the employees are distinctly American. Employees address each other by their first names. The dress code is more casual. All of this signifies a much more relaxed environment inherent in the movie-making industry where creativity reigns over process. Employees there, even expatriates sent from Japan, say that it is hard to believe that the owner of the company is Japanese. Nevertheless, Sony holds on dearly to the notion of familial loyalty and responsibility. From the minute new employees step through the doors of Sony Corporation, they are welcomed to the family and told: "Expect to work very hard and we will repay you with security and our gratitude." Just like the relationship between father and son, brother and sister, the relationship between the Sony employee and the company is valued more highly than a mere financial transaction.

Sony's family spirit cascades down the entire corporation, from the chairman to the lowliest worker on the factory floor, giving everyone a sense that the company is the property of the employees, not just of a few top people. The people at the top of the company feel that they have a responsibility to lead this family company and express concerns about its members. One of the ways in which the founders tried to foster this kind of solidarity within the entire company was the Sony jacket. The jacket was partly inspired by the Mao jackets in communist China. Grey, with red piping, the jacket is given to everyone in the Sony family, in Japan and wherever there is a Sony presence. Up until his death in December 1997,

Ibuka was known to wear his jacket often at Sony headquarters as a way to show that he was just another member of the same Sony family. There is a constant tug between Sony's core Japanese management philosophy and its quirky bits of Western corporate culture, which we will discuss more in the next chapter.

ORIGIN OF THE SONY JACKET

When Morita and Ibuka started the company, clothing was scarce and expensive on the black market. People came to work in an odd assortment of gear: returning soldiers wore bits of their uniform or old-fashioned suits that had been saved for many years. If a person was fortunate enough to have a good suit, he didn't want to wear it to the office where he might risk soiling it or burning a hole in it with acid. But some of Sony's employees didn't have the money to invest in a work jacket. So, with company money, the founders bought a jacket for everyone to wear in the office. Soon these jackets became a symbol of the Sony family. Morita even got renowned Japanese designer Issey Miyake to design a jacket for the company. As the company prospered, management could have done away with the jackets (there were summer and winter models) because everyone was better paid and could afford their own clothing, but everybody seemed to like the idea of the jacket, and so Sony continued to provide them.

SPEAK UP

To a Japanese corporate culture meticulously aware of hierarchies and formalities, Sony's culture of encouraging its employees to be independent-minded and speak up is almost irreverent. Management consultants who have worked closely with Sony executives and employees and have sat through countless hours of Sony's strategy meetings recount their initial surprise when they noticed that everyone speaks their mind at these discussion groups. "Everyone, as part of the Sony family, is expected to speak up when they have something to say. If you don't speak up, it actually reflects poorly on you and your performance review," says one consultant who has worked closely with Sony for years. Although there is an inherent understanding that the top managers have the final say and direct Sony's vision and strategies, there is at least a very conscious attempt within Sony's corporate culture to eliminate any class divide or bureaucratic hierarchy. Every member of the family matters. Top managers in the company set a clear example of this, and of how expressing an opinion — and perhaps a disagreement with a corporate decision — won't necessarily result in a demotion or firing, and may lead to reward. "At our company, we are challenged to bring our ideas out into the open. If they clash with others, so much the better, because out of it may come something good at a higher level," Morita wrote in his autobiography.

Ken Kutaragi, father of the Sony PlayStation (the PlayStation story will be detailed in Chapter 4), is a prime example to illustrate this aspect of Sony culture. A bright engineer, Kutaragi had a dream of making a computer-game console, believing that Sony, with its technology and innovative spirit, could easily outsmart long-time veterans in the industry. Kutaragi's proposal was met with great opposition, mostly by critics who believed that Sony shouldn't enter a new and unfamiliar industry when it was already doing well with its electronics business. Kutaragi insisted and, eventually, Ohga gave him the green light to pursue the project, now one of Sony's most profitable divisions.

INTERNAL MOBILITY

The idea of family also includes the company's responsibility to take care of its employees and offer them opportunities to grow. Sony motivates its employees through a program called the internal mobility system. A weekly company newsletter advertises job openings throughout the Sony group. Workers are encouraged to try new jobs for which they qualify and that interest them. This way, employees don't feel stuck in their jobs. There is also a performance review for employees every six months to help them evaluate their performance and trace a career path they wish to follow. An engineer who has been in the design center for 25 years may decide he wants to try working in marketing or corporate communications. If his qualifications match and an opening is available, an engineer who spent his entire Sony career designing machines could almost overnight become a media spokesman for the company or a marketing guru. The same applies for employees who wish to take advantage of Sony's global network and get postings abroad. (But employees overseas who want to move to Japan must be able to communicate in Japanese.)

Sony has taken risks with its hiring, with a view to finding talented employees. This approach may be the legacy of Sony's origins as a young company competing against established conglomerates. It has had to poach experienced engineers and marketers from other companies, as well as tap college graduates and young entrepreneurs with the potential and energy to move up through the ranks, as we saw earlier with the examples of Ohga and Idei.

ONE FOR ALL AND ALL FOR ONE

"At our company, we are challenged to bring our ideas out into the open. If they clash with others, so much the better, because out of it may come something good at a higher level." — Akio Morita, founder

When Sony introduced a series of commercials and advertisements with the slogan, "Do you dream in Sony?", the thinking behind the pitch was to get consumers to buy Sony — the whole brand and the whole lifestyle; from its Walkmans to its VCRs to its televisions to its camcorders. Just as Sony wants consumers to live in its world, it invites its employees to do the same by creating this very familial web, which brews loyalty, trust and commitment from both the institution and the individuals. In this almost-protectionist formula, the creative element and the risk-taking attitude is not entirely lost. Largely, the secret to Sony's success lies in its founders' vision and unequivocal belief in the company — as a family, as a risk-taking innovative engine, as a new kind of entrepreneurial company that breaks the mold. The two believed in starting something new, and building it little by little in a Japanese business environment dominated and overwhelmed by century-old conglomerates.

It was both Morita's charisma and Ibuka's enthusiasm and belief in the potential of technological advancements that laid the foundation of a company built on trust, loyalty and adventure. The dynamic between the two co-founders demonstrated how their strengths complemented each other and how two people from different walks of life could come together and work side by side almost like brothers.

When they were both at work, Ibuka and Morita took lunch together. If Ibuka and Morita had serious disagreements over the years, they resolved them privately. Regarding company policy, they spoke with one voice; no one in or outside Sony ever heard either of them criticize the other openly. Everyone, including the founders' children and spouses, who saw them together has remarked on the exclusive bond that united them in a mysterious way.

There were moments of discord, generally when the pragmatic and business-minded Morita clashed with the impulsive and naïve Ibuka. Most of the anecdotes are trivial, remembered only because they were rare. Even when, in the early 1960s, Morita was desperately anxious to cut losses because of Sony's unsuccessful attempts to develop the Chromatron electron beam that would produce color for Sony televisions, there was never concern that he would stop Ibuka. For Morita, interfering with a plan conceived by his senior partner, obstructing his dream or vision, or in any way disappointing whatever desire he chose to entertain, however childish or irrational, was unthinkable. On the contrary, applying his persuasiveness to help Ibuka's visions come to life was in the nature of the relationship.

With the founders' era now winding down at Sony, the company's top executives would still echo the founders' relationship and their management philosophies when addressing staff, or motivating their engineers when embarking on a new project. As one Sony executive describes it: "The founders' behavior and managerial styles are still bible for our current management."

SONY'S RECIPES FOR SUCCESS

- *Company equals second family*: Treat your employees as you would family members, offering them trust, job security and career development, and a promise of healthy compensation, and they will reciprocate with loyalty and hard work. This tight connection between employer and employee has been a main factor in explaining why Sony's groomed executives seldom leave the company for a competitor.

- *Mistakes are okay*: While individual accountability is important, encouraging employees to take measured risks is equally vital in the quest of innovation and discovery. Sometimes with risks, mistakes happen. Instead of immediately taking punitive action against employees for their mistakes, try to find the cause of the mistake. At Sony, the belief is that if you can learn from your mistakes and improve on your work — whether it be inventions or marketing campaigns — then you are a better person because of that, and there's no need to punish.

- *Speak your mind*: Allowing employees to express their opinions and voice their criticisms is a crucial part of a corporation's self-improvement process. This requires an environment that encourages the open expression of views and opinions unhindered by the fear of retribution or punishment.

- *Make career development possible*: Allowing room for employees to grow within the corporate structure is vital to keeping turnover low and employees' morale high. This might include offering employees opportunities to work in different kinds of jobs, exposing them to new business cultures through overseas postings and giving them a sense that they have a long and prosperous future at the company.

NOTES

Consultants interviewed for the book all declined to be named. Most of them still work on projects with Sony and felt it would be inappropriate to comment on the record about the company.

1. John Nathan, *Sony: The Private Life*, Mariner Books, 1999.

2. Simon Partner, *Assembled in Japan: Electrical Goods And The Making of The Japanese Consumer*, University of California Press, 1999.

3. *Genryu*, Sony Corporation of America, 1996.
    Other information — general and specific — is from the Sony corporate website (www.sony.net) and from interviews with Mack Araki, Kei Sakaguchi, Masanobu Sakaguchi and Takehito Soeda, Sony employees in the U.S.

4. James C. Abegglen, *Kaisha, the Japanese Corporation*, Basic Books, 1985.

5. Akio Morita, Edwin M. Reingold and Mitsuko Shimomura, *Made In Japan: Akio Morita and Sony*, William Collins Sons & Co. Ltd., 1987.

Two

MOVING BEYOND THE HOME FRONT: INTERNATIONALIZATION

In 1961, Sony became the first Japanese company to offer its stock in the United States. In 1971, it became the first to build a factory there. And today, it is one of the few Japanese companies to have outsiders on its Board of Directors. This chapter explores the calculations and strategies that have made Sony a globally recognized brand.

I n the summer of 1990, Norio Ohga, then president of Sony Corporation, was reviewing the company's fiscal year financial performance. It had been a banner year. Sales had increased 34 per cent, to US$18 billion, and net income had increased 42 per cent, to $655 million, both record levels for the company. Sony had registered strong growth across all product areas in all major markets around the world. It had also completed a significant expansion of its business through two major acquisitions: CBS Records Inc. and Columbia TriStar Pictures. These acquisitions established a significant position for the company in all aspects of the entertainment field, including both hardware and software. Top management felt that such a position was key to providing the necessary synergy between content and electronics to ensure continued leadership in product development.

With such a phenomenal financial year behind him, Ohga weighed the challenges that still lay ahead for the company at the time. Sony's rapid expansion prompted him to consider how to manage the corporation's worldwide growth and how to achieve a smooth and full integration of its diverse activities. In this vein, Ohga was specifically concerned about how to incorporate Sony's newly acquired music and movie businesses into the U.S. operations, a critical component of the corporation's global strategy.

Ohga's dilemma was one that multinational corporations faced daily in this increasingly interconnected business world:

How should the company preserve its overall corporate culture and values when expanding beyond the home-base culture? At the same time, how does it gain the trust and understanding of consumers in new business communities and cultures?

ANYTHING IS POSSIBLE

Being global is intuitive for Sony. From the selecting of its name to its careful product planning, Sony is constantly keeping the consumers in mind — and consumers as a whole are not restricted by geographical boundaries. Perhaps, in this regard, Sony's ethos arose from it being a Japanese company and having a limited consumer market at home. Perhaps the post-war U.S. occupation of Japan showed the company's founders a glimpse of the possibilities beyond their boundaries. Perhaps it was the ambition and entrepreneurial spirit of Ibuka and Morita themselves that gave rise to this worldview. Whatever the reason, it seemed as though the founders always had globalization in their plans for the company. In 1952, Sony had launched a successful tape-recorder business and Ibuka visited the U.S. to see what uses were being made of the tape. Although that portion of the trip turned out to be disappointing, Ibuka learned about a device called the transistor, which had been invented at Bell Laboratories. He and Morita had been toying with the idea of making a high-frequency radio and it seemed like the transistor could play a part in this.

Morita went to New York in 1953 to talk to Bell Lab about possibly purchasing the license on its transistor technology. But getting the necessary permission from the Japanese

Ministry of International Trade and Industry (MITI) to purchase the license on the transistor was no easy matter. MITI officials didn't believe that such a small company could possibly undertake the enormous task of dealing with brand-new foreign technologies and were opposed to the proposed purchase. It took six months of lobbying before Morita was able to go to New York to finalize the purchase.

The purchase of transistor technology was successful, and Sony introduced its first transistorized radio in 1955 and the first pocket-sized radio in 1957. But the more important revelation on Morita's 1953 trip was that he got to see the world and the infinite opportunities for Sony to grow in this global market. On the way back from New York to Tokyo, Morita made stops in Europe, visiting established business powerhouses such as Volkswagen, Mercedes and Siemens, and other smaller companies, some of which have disappeared in the ensuing years. In the electronics field, Morita paid a visit to Royal Philips Electronics in Holland, which had already established its reputation worldwide.

> "If a man born in such a small, out-of-the-way place in an agricultural country could build such a huge, highly technical company with a fine worldwide reputation like Philips, maybe, just maybe, Sony could do the same thing in Japan."
> — Akio Morita, founder

In Germany, Morita found the country's rapid post-war recovery impressive. One day, he ordered some ice cream in a restaurant on Koenigsstrasse in Dusseldorf, and the waiter served it with a miniature paper parasol stuck into it as decoration. "This is from your country," he said, smiling, to Morita, probably intending it to be a compliment.

"That was the extent of his knowledge of Japan and its capabilities," Morita wrote in his autobiography. "What a long way we had to go!"[1]

Discouraged by the waiter's comments, Morita arrived in Eindhoven, Holland, where Philips was headquartered. Eindhoven was the polar opposite of the industrial feel of Germany. It was a purely agricultural country, and a small one at that. There were old-fashioned windmills everywhere, just as could be seen in old Dutch landscape paintings. It surprised Morita that the great Philips Electronics enterprise would be located in a small town in a small corner of a small agricultural country. "I stared at the statue of Dr. Philips in front of the train station, and I thought of our own village of Kosugaya and the similar bronze statue of my father's great-grandfather that once stood there," he wrote, and he drew inspiration from this. He quickly wrote Ibuka from Eindhoven, and this was the gist of his message: If a man born in such a small, out-of-the-way place in an agricultural country could build such a huge, highly technical company with a fine worldwide reputation like Philips, maybe, just maybe, Sony could do the same thing in Japan.

WHAT'S IN A NAME?

On the same visit to the U.S. in 1953, Morita realized another thing: no one could pronounce the company's name, Tokyo Tsushin Kogyo. Even the nickname, Totsuko, was a tongue twister, difficult for foreigners to remember. So the founders decided they needed to change their name. The company would stand a much better chance of being recognized if they could come up with something ingenious. They first considered changing the name to Tokyo Teletech, but then they learned that there was an American company that used the name Teletech. Whatever new name they came up with, it had to serve double duty as both the company name and the brand name, and thus reduce the amount they would have to spend on advertising to make both well known.

With Teletech a non-starter, Morita and Ibuka toyed with designing a corporate symbol — an inverted pyramid inside a thin circle with small wedges cut from the sides of the pyramid to give a stylized letter "T." But the co-founders weren't satisfied. They were looking for something special, especially now that they were making radios with transistor technology, which the Americans who sold them the license hadn't believed was possible. The new name would have to be something everyone could remember because the transistor radio would be the first product bearing this brand name.[2]

When Morita was in the U.S., he noticed that many companies were using three letter logotypes, such as ABC, NBC, RCA, and AT&T. Others were using their full name. Morita liked that concept. He remembered that when he was a boy he learned to recognize the names of imported automobiles by their symbols — the three-pointed star for Mercedes, the blue oval with Ford in it, the Cadillac crown, the Pierce arrow, the Winged Victory of Rolls-Royce. Later, many car companies, such as Chevrolet, Ford and Buick, began to use their names in conjunction with the symbol.

Ibuka and Morita decided that they didn't want a corporate symbol. The name itself would be the symbol, so it had to be short. At the time, Japanese companies typically had a company badge and a lapel pin, usually in the shape of the company symbol. But, with few exceptions (the three diamonds of Mitsubishi, being one), the link between the corporate symbol and the corporation brand was rarely clear to the outsider. Like the automobile companies that began to rely less on symbols and more on their names, Ibuka and Morita felt they really needed a catchy and meaningful name to carry the message. They wanted a new name that could be recognized anywhere in the world, one that could be pronounced the same in any language. They went through the dictionaries, looking for a name with a ring, and came across the Latin word *sonus*, which means "sound". Transistor radios were sound equipment; the word *sonus* seemed fitting for what they were looking for. So they homed in on the Latin word.

At the time, borrowed English slang and nicknames were becoming popular in Japan, partly because of the American occupation. Some people referred to bright, young, cute boys as "sonny", or "sonny-boys". "Sunny" and "sonny" both had an optimistic and bright sound similar to the Latin root with which the founders were working. Sony engineers considered themselves "sonny-boys" because they felt they were part of a new kind of company, one with an entrepreneurial soul. Unfortunately, "sonny" on its own would give the company trouble in Japan because, in the Romanization of the Japanese language, the word "sonny" would be pronounced "sohn-nee", which means "to lose money" — not the luckiest name for an upstart trying to establish a solid reputation. The solution to this particular concern struck Morita one day: why not just drop one of the letters and make it "Sony"? And that was how the name of this Japanese consumer-electronics giant came to be.

The new name had the advantage of carrying no meaning but itself in any language. It was easy to remember, and it had the connotations the founders were looking for. Because it was written in Roman letters, people in many countries could think of it as being in their own language. All over the world, governments were spending money to teach people how to read English and use the Roman alphabet. The more people who learned English and the Roman alphabet, the logic goes, the more people would recognize the Sony name and company at no cost to the company.

ONWARD AND OUTWARD TO CONQUER THE WORLD

When the first transistor radio made its debut in 1955, the co-founders thought it would be only logical to sell it first in the market in which they had bought the know-how. If Sony succeeded in the U.S., it could bring back that success to Japan, and then spread out to Europe and other countries.

This was an early thinking at Sony — to seek out foreign markets for its products. Even though Sony was a Tokyo-based company, the founders always sensed that consumers were not bound by geographical limits, so neither should Sony. And Sony would soon learn to develop its own distribution and marketing system, limiting its dependence on third-party distributors where it could.

UNDERSTAND OTHER CULTURES

The challenge for companies wishing to globalize is often cultural rather than strategic. Understanding how business is done in other cultures, and how the company can fit into the local communities, is a crucial part of succeeding outside the home territory.

- *Hire locally:* learn from local managers who have the experience and understanding of how business is done in their home countries. They can guide you through negotiations with local governments, strike deals with suppliers and distributors and help ease your company into the fabric of the local communities.

- *Strike a balance between your home culture and local culture:* One of the biggest challenges for Sony in the U.S. early on was maneuvering through the American product-distribution system while trying to preserve the autonomy and brand image of the company's products. Sony established its own distribution system but worked closely with American retailers to educate them about the Sony brand and products so that these retailers would be able to convey the Sony spirit fully to consumers.

- *Participate in the local community:* Similar to the principle of hiring locally, a key component to expanding abroad is to blend into the local community. This could be done by listing the company on the local stock exchange, participating in community service projects, appointing well-respected local executives to your Board of Directors, among other things.

The first transistor radio was small and practical and Morita believed that it was a viable product to market to the U.S. The American economy was booming, employment was high, people were progressive and eager for new things, and international travel was becoming easier. So, in 1955, Morita took a $29.95 radio to New York and made the rounds of possible retailers. Much to his surprise, many retailers were unimpressed. They told him, "Why are you making such tiny radios? Everybody in American wants big radios. We have big houses, plenty of room. Who needs these tiny things?"

Morita was eventually able to find a like-minded distributor in Delmonico International, which became Sony's first distributor in the United States. But it wasn't long before that relationship started to erode. As Sony's name became better known and sales increased, Morita felt that the people at Delmonico seemed more interested in low price than in quality. It got to the point where Morita found himself haggling with Delmonico executives over the cost of the imitation-leather case, and whether Sony could make it a few cents cheaper. They also asked Sony to produce some inexpensive radios that they could sell at high volume at big discounts. But that was not the Sony style, and Morita told them so. Sony's corporate mission was to bring useful, imaginative products to consumers, not to produce low-quality goods just to make a buck. This difference in philosophy would later create irreparable tensions between Sony and Delmonico.

In 1959, when Sony announced to the world that it had succeeded in making the world's first transistorized television set, Delmonico, without consulting Sony, began advertising that they would be handling it. Before the ink was dry on the ad campaign, Morita informed Delmonico that he had no intention of marketing television sets through them. He wanted to preserve an image of class and high quality. This was the last straw that broke the short-lived relationship. Realizing that other dealers and retailers would not value the

Sony name and the hard work that went into building products bearing that name, Morita came to the conclusion that Sony would, for the sake of protecting the brand name, have to develop its own, independent, distribution system.

At this point, Morita was traveling between Tokyo and New York several times each month. As executive vice-president, he really couldn't afford to be away from Tokyo for long, but as a man overseeing U.S. operations, he couldn't afford to spend too much time in Tokyo either. So he decided that Sony had to establish firmer roots in the U.S. The company had to understand the Americans better if it were to establish its name there. In the late 1950s, more than half of Sony's production was already going abroad. The future of the company would depend to a great extent on the U.S. and on other international business.

So Morita proposed the establishment of a U.S. unit of Sony. Many of his colleagues, including Ibuka and Kazuo Iwama, were skeptical of this idea, not to mention the small cadre of employees and executives Morita assembled in New York. But Morita was convinced that having Sony's very own U.S. office was the right thing to do. Sony would be able to set up its own sales network, be its own distributor, and develop its own expertise in marketing. Nobody could come up with very good reasons why they shouldn't do it.

For some time, Sony had been waiting on permission from the Ministry of Finance to remit US$500,000 to the United States for future use there. Coincidentally, the permission came through just around the time Morita was making his pitch for a new American company. So, in February 1960, Sony officially established its American division, Sony Corporation of America.[3]

Sixteen months later, Sony offered two million shares of its common stock in the U.S. market as American Depository Receipts (ADR). Although Tokyo Electric Power Company had issued bonds in the U.S. market before the Second World War, Sony was the first Japanese company to offer its stock in the United States, issuing a total of five million ADRs on two occasions (1961 and 1963), which raised approximately ¥4 billion.

On September 17, 1970, Morita and Noboru Yoshii of Sony were welcomed to the first floor of the New York Stock Exchange (NYSE) by its chairman, 30 minutes prior to the opening of the trading day. At that time, NYSE handled 75 per cent (in value) of the world's stocks. A decade after it first opened its doors to America, Sony had fulfilled all the qualifications required for listing on the NYSE, becoming the 1,305[th] firm (and the 30th non-U.S. firm and the first Japanese firm) to be welcomed to the world's largest stock exchange. This was the day Sony management had long been waiting for.

At exactly 10 a.m., the bells announcing the opening of trade rang. In accordance with NYSE tradition, Morita immediately bought 100 Sony ADRs in his own name. As soon as this order was sent to the back office the opening price flashed across the electronic bulletin board: "SNE $15 5/8". Morita and Yoshii joyfully held the ticker tape with this price on it.[4]

What did listing on the New York Stock Exchange mean?

It was a show of recognition of Sony's status as a truly international company, and a nod to Morita and Ibuka that part of their vision of creating a global company had been symbolically fulfilled. The listing also symbolically affirmed that Sony was now elevated to the same playing field as industry giants such as General Motors Corp., whose sales at the time exceeded the Japanese national budget. Sony stocks were bought nonstop that first day. The closing price was $15 1/4; trading volume was 120,300 shares, putting them in 13th place among the total 1,305 companies listed. At the press briefing that day, Morita announced enthusiastically, "Sony has just taken its first step toward becoming an global company. We intend to list in European markets as well, building Sony up to becoming an international company with global foundations." By 1977, Sony was listed on 18 major exchanges in 10 countries. Sony stocks are now being traded in some corner of the world virtually 24 hours a day.

TOUCH EVERY CORNER

When Morita and Ibuka decided that they wanted Sony to be a global company, they really weren't kidding. And they weren't talking just about the obvious markets in the U.S. and Europe. In the 1960s, not long after Sony began operating in Europe and the United States, the company placed a rather unusual advertisement in the *Asahi Shimbun*, one of Japan's leading national newspapers. The headline read: "Wanted: People Capable of Arguing in English". The advertisement, as it turned out, was placed for the recruitment of staff for its overseas operations.

Hajime Unoki was one of the many who came Sony's way. He left his trading company job in 1959 to join Sony as one of its first employees in the newly created International Division. (His father had actually taken the liberty of sending an application form to Sony on his behalf.) Several months later, he found he was to be sent to Africa, with Morita urging him to "Go as soon as possible. Africa is calling you." But this was easier said than done. Most African nations at the time were still under the jurisdiction of the United Kingdom and other countries, and Unoki was told that it would take up to three months to get visas for the countries he wanted to visit. He couldn't afford to wait that long. Fortunately, the newly independent Egypt had just established an embassy in Toyko. Unoki applied for a visa and it was processed on the spot. He left for Egypt soon after with a bag full of sample transistor radios, figuring that he would find his way around once he got to the African continent.

After landing in Cairo, he eventually got visas and traveled to Sudan, Ethiopia, Kenya, Uganda, Tanganyika, Rhodesia, South Africa and several West African countries. In total, Unoki spent roughly six months in Africa. His assignment was to find potential distributors. Based on the research he had done on the companies that had made inquiries to Sony, he compiled a list of potential partners. Once on location, he conducted further research on the business operations and financial status of these firms at banks and the local chambers of commerce. If the figures and the storefronts looked promising, he simply telephoned the potential client and said, "I'm here. May I come and see you?"

Unoki wrote letters to Tokyo daily, reporting on the stores he had visited, the feasibility of doing business with them, and his impressions of the stores and people. He seldom received any replies because the many places he visited had no reliable sources of electricity. In such circumstances, a transistor radio operating on a small battery proved incredibly popular. Unoki found that as soon as he presented his samples to potential distributors, they all wanted to start doing business with Sony right away. Business with dealers like Tedelex of South Africa, with which Sony has maintained a relationship for more than 30 years, began just this way.

THINK GLOBALLY, ACT LOCALLY

Of late, "localization" has been a buzzword among multinational companies. In the consumer goods and services industries, Western companies are trying to capture the hearts of Asian consumers, whose interests and tastes sometimes differ wildly from those of Westerners, whether it be the flavor of beverage they like, the shampoo they use or the food they eat. "Think globally, act locally" has been hailed by business professors and consultants alike as the key that will turn a buck in diverse emerging markets.

Since Sony first began opening its overseas offices, it has been localizing. For a consumer-electronics company, localization is a vital part of the business strategy. Consumers around the world may all need televisions and radios and tape recorders and other gadgets, but how much do they want to pay? Who do you appeal to with new products? How do you inspire interest in a new concept? Sony prides itself on creating products it believes consumers would want, rather than relying on consumers to say "We need better televisions" and so on. Sony often used Japan, its home turf, as a test market for its new products. But how can you be sure that the tastes and interests of an American or European consumer will be the same as those of a Japanese consumer? Sometimes they are and sometimes they're not. Sony found this out quickly when it first introduced its VAIO computers to the U.S. Some of the models, equipped with sound- and video-editing functions, were wildly popular in Japan. But when they landed in the U.S., the interest was slim. Why? It wasn't because consumers didn't admire the functions of the VAIO computer. Many simply felt these computers, priced at $1,700 and up, were way out of their price range. Unlike in Japan where VAIO computers as a whole captured close to half of the PC market, in the U.S., the market share hovers at about 15 per cent and in Europe even less. It takes someone on the ground in Los Angeles or London or Berlin to know how consumers there behave and how they will react to a new product. That is part of what localization is about — market knowledge, cultural understanding, business expertise.

Sony's localization strategy is two-fold. On the most basic level, it has localized the operational side — everything from sales, distribution and production to research and development. This has meant having offices in the countries in which it is selling products, or at least within close proximity of its consumers in a specific region. Round that out with a smart group of local executives, and you have a second level of localization.

The challenge then lies in achieving both levels of localization well. Sony has tweaked the structure of its global operations almost every decade, reshuffling different business units in order to achieve localization most efficiently and effectively.

LOCALIZE OPERATIONS

In the early 1970s, Sony began to see the potential for increased trade friction between Japan and other countries, which could in turn affect its plans to expand its international business. One early warning sign was a May 1970 *Time* magazine article titled "Japan Invasion?", in which Sony had featured. Morita, deeply concerned about protecting

Sony's good reputation in the United States, decided to take action to remedy this misperception. First, in 1971, the company built a color-television plant in the U.S. Second, in 1972, Morita hired Harvey Schein as president of Sony's American operations, instituting a policy within the corporation of, where appropriate, putting a local in the leadership position.

Schein, a Harvard Law School graduate and former president of CBS's Record Division, had a reputation as a tough executive. In order to attract him, the company offered an annual salary in excess of $200,000, far more than that of any other Sony executive, with the exception of Morita. Schein accepted the position, with two conditions. First, the U.S. operations had the right to import. Second, the U.S. operation had to be a profit center. Schein proceeded to install modern U.S. management systems, including strict budgeting and formal planning systems, and also instituted aggressive programs to hire good local staff. Many Japanese who worked under him and went on to become senior executives have referred to him as a "great trainer".

Around the same time, during the 1970s, local executives were hired at Sony's European operations and given full authority and responsibility for running their business units. However, policies and operating procedures for managing these rapidly growing international operations were lacking. Localization centered on each individual country, with each operation dealing directly and independently of one another with headquarters in Tokyo. There was little, if any, coordination or cooperation among subsidiaries, even within the same region.

As Schein continued to build a more autonomous operation, it became a growing concern to the headquarters. Following tough price negotiations between the U.S. marketing organization and the plants in Japan for transfer prices in the early part of the 1970s, there was little further involvement from the Japanese parent as to how the U.S. units should strategize or operate. Because of the importance of the American business to the total company, the local operation was becoming too powerful and independent, and not heeding directives from Japan. Headquarters complained that Schein was taking a short-term outlook and not recognizing the need to invest in the market. Conflicts over specific investments (such as in its video business) continued to grow; philosophies over how to manage a business continued to clash. Eventually, in 1978, Schein resigned.

GLOCALIZATION, MORITA STYLE

In the late 1970s, the company began to consider that its localization efforts had gone too far. All the operations were running too independently of each other and especially of the parent company in Tokyo. In 1977, on his return to Japan from the U.S., Ken Iwaki established a corporate planning department at headquarters to introduce a more central coordination of activities. In addition, Sony set up the International Operations Committee, composed of top executives from key operations throughout the world, which met twice a year. (A similar kind of structure exists now where top executives from key subsidiaries and operations around the world meet at least once a year to discuss the Sony group business strategy.)

COMMUNICATE WELL

Once you've established operations abroad, the challenge then becomes how to manage these operations. How much leeway should they get independent of directives from headquarters? How much control should headquarters exert on these overseas operations? Too much control, and you may stifle the growth of overseas operations. Too little oversight, and they may undermine the brand integrity of the corporation. Communication becomes crucial here.

- *International operations committee*: Comprising top executives from key operations throughout the world, this committee can be a good forum for executives to exchange intelligence about their countries' business environments and discuss the changes in the global economy. Top executives of the parent corporation could also offer an overview of the company's business strategies for the near and long term, so that all the operations can synchronize their plans with the corporate vision.

- *Marketing council*: Sub-committees such as a marketing council can allow executives from different business units to work together better to promote products and services for the company. Business units can tie in product and services launches with one another. For example, a new mobile-phone marketing campaign can be linked to the promotion of a new film, using characters from the movie to advertise the new phone product.

- *Set up regional headquarters*: On a daily basis, it is probably unnecessary and even inefficient for headquarters to be involved in every decision a local country operation makes. That is why regional headquarters become a useful corporate structure to ensure that lines of communication are open at all times. Regional headquarters, organized typically according to the

> major regions of the world, Asia, the Americas, Europe and Africa (although some companies break it down more finely), have both the understanding about the local cultures of their regions and a broader perspective than the individual country operations, and can serve as the solid middleman between local operations and headquarters.

Throughout the 1980s, Sony embarked on an evolution of its corporate structure through an approach described by top management as "global localization". In order to bring independently minded overseas operations under central control, the company introduced the concept of strategic business units (SBUs), giving the new units full accountability for a business on a global basis. In 1983, there were six SBUs, a number which increased to 16 in 1989.

Each SBU was asked to reduce manufacturing costs by more than the traditional 10 per cent annual targets. Country managers were asked to improve efficiency in their respective operations. By 1985, the company had completed a global production plan based on three regions: Japan and the rest of Asia; the United States and Canada; and Europe. Several targets for 1990 were established, including reducing the percentage of total production done in Japan from 80 per cent to 50 per cent, with the balance shared 15 per cent to 20 per cent each in the U.S, Europe, and the rest of Asia. To implement this strategy, the idea was that local support, including logistics, quality assurance, and parts supply, would be established wherever Sony had a presence, and that finance, general administration and data processing would be strengthened at a regional level.

THE ORIGINS OF "GLOCALIZATION" (GLOBAL LOCALIZATION)

In March 1988, in Rome, Sony's top managers were discussing "globalization" issues with European executives. Somebody commented that what was being discussed wasn't in fact globalization, but localization, because production was being shifted from Japan to Europe, and parts procurement, design engineering, and other support functions were to be localized. Morita agreed, mentioning that he would prefer localization to globalization. Then, suddenly, an idea seemed to have struck him. He said, "Let's call it 'global localization' because today's localization is different from that of 10 years ago. Today's localization must be well positioned and coordinated from a global strategic point of view."

At both the May 1988 General Management Conference and the International Top Management Meeting in July of that year, Morita, then chairman, introduced a new principle. "Each of our regional headquarters in Japan, the U.S., Europe and Asia," he said, "must set new goals to localize operations. This process must be conducted in accordance with the unified goal of making Sony a truly global company. I would thus like to introduce the principle of 'global localization' as our future guiding principle. This is a new way of life for Sony, whereby we meet local needs with local operations while following common global concepts and technologies."

In the mid 1980s, the rising value of the yen affected Sony greatly. In a period of three years, the yen went from ¥250 to US$1, in 1985, to ¥120 to US$1 in 1988. In 1986, in dollar-terms, sales increased 24 per cent but, in yen, they dropped 11 per cent. As a result of these pressures, worldwide operating income fell 75 per cent. Even rival Matsushita, whose dependence on foreign markets was not as high as Sony's, had its operating income fall by 44 per cent. At the time, approximately 70 per cent of Sony's sales were from outside Japan. These trends highlighted the urgent need for Sony to expand its manufacturing operations outside Japan. By 1990, more than 30 per cent of Sony's total production occurred outside Japan, with manufacturing operations in 17 countries.

It really wasn't until the 1990s that Sony felt that it had fully achieved true globalization, largely grounded in the idea that each region of its worldwide operations would have a headquarters from which to implement the company's vision.

Sony began with Europe. With the unification of the EC scheduled for 1992, Sony Europe G.m.b.H. was established in Germany in November 1986 as a self-contained operation under Jakob J. Schmuckli, former president of Sony Deutschland G.m.b.H. In 1987, the then vice-president Masaaki Morita, the co-founder's brother, moved to the U.S. as chairman and CEO of Sony Corporation of America. His mission was to restructure the corporation to strengthen the U.S. manufacturing and engineering base. That same year, Sony decided to establish Sony International (Singapore) Ltd., its regional headquarters for Asia (excluding Japan).

These operational headquarters were given the authority to make decisions regarding production, sales, logistics, technology and financing to maximize operational efficiency and meet regional needs. The company's Tokyo headquarters served as the manager of the Japanese domestic market, and oversaw the entire global operation. Japan would continue to function as the primary center for R&D and the development of new production technology. It would also coordinate future activities so that the four regional headquarters would complement each other to realize a global collaboration that maximized resources.

BEYOND THE U.S.

In 1959, Sony opened its first European office in Zurich. The following year, this office was expanded and incorporated as Sony Overseas S.A. (SOSA). This sales company began with just four employees, including a Swiss secretary. Once Sony Corporation of America (SONAM or SCA for short) and SOSA were up and running, daily contact with the Tokyo-based International Division was maintained by telex to agree on production and sales quantities. Aside from SOSA and SCA, Sony's two other overseas operations in the early 1960s were the Hong Kong office, established in 1958, and a production plant in Ireland, established in 1959. There was not even one representative office outside the United States and Europe. Members of the new International Division took turns taking two-to-three-month trips to establish local distribution channels and conduct market research.

In those days, Japanese people going abroad were still so rare that they were seen off by big groups of well-wishers shouting "Banzai!" for good luck at the airport. The names of employees traveling abroad and returning to Japan were all listed in the "Overseas Travelers" column of the weekly company newsletter, founded in 1960 to facilitate internal communications.

In more recent years, the boom of the China market and the rapid growth of Sony's Asian business has reduced Singapore's role as a regional headquarters. Singapore now oversees Malaysia, Indonesia and the Southeast Asian countries. Sony (China) Ltd. was established to manage the growing market there. Elsewhere, changes in global economics and the increasing interconnectedness of the business world are also altering the structure of the regional headquarters. For now, Berlin and New York remain headquarters for the European and North American regions respectively. But there is no doubt Sony will tweak its global corporate structure as the tide of globalization takes its course.

INNOVATE ACROSS BORDERS

From the beginning, Morita and Ibuka placed an emphasis on research and development (R&D) to develop the new technologies and products. Traditionally, these R&D activities were centered in Japan. In the late 1980s, as part of its globalization policy, Sony began to expand its overseas R&D facilities to complement its growing manufacturing presences around the globe. This expansion was necessary in order to shorten the development cycle and to make better use of global R&D capabilities.

In May 1989, the Advanced Video Technology Center (AVTC), the development base for HDTV (high-definition television) in the U.S., was constructed in San Jose, California. At the opening ceremony, Morita said, "We believe it is necessary to develop products locally in order to meet the needs and requirements of the local market. Also, if we could transfer such local specialties as digital technologies of the United Kingdom or graphics and special effects technologies of the U.S. to other regions, we would realize a global synergy in R&D."

The message behind Morita's speech was that global localization as the new guiding corporate concept for the future of Sony would also apply to R&D and include technology transfers from one regional R&D center to another. Moreover, like marketing and manufacturing, R&D would be conducted close to Sony's end markets. "My First Sony", for example, a series of products aimed at young children, was an idea first generated in the United States. The total time from concept to production was 12 months, very short by industry standards, thanks to the new take on how Sony could leverage its talented engineers, marketers, and thinkers in all corners of the world. By 1990, in the United States, Sony operated three technology centers and had plans for further expansion. In Europe, between 1988 and 1990, technology centers were also established in Germany and the U.K.

"We believe it is necessary to develop products locally in order to meet the needs and requirements of the local market. Also, if we could transfer such local specialties as digital technologies of the United Kingdom or graphics and special effects technologies of the U.S. to other regions, we would realize a global synergy in R&D."
— Akio Morita, founder

For many years, Sony has been conducting technological development abroad for broadcast and industrial applications. The first such center was Sony Broadcast Ltd. (SBC), established in the United Kingdom in 1978. Since then, SBC has been conducting sales and marketing of broadcast equipment, while pursuing broadcast systems design and R&D projects. The SBC R&D team developed the first broadcast-use digital-component VTR through a joint-development project with Atsugi-based Sony researchers. One example of cross-national technology-development coordination is Sony's broadcasting systems, including HDTV. For this project, Sony involved four R&D labs around the world. The main laboratory was the development facility in Atsugi, Japan, where the company had its core hardware capability. The company also involved development laboratories in San Jose, California, Basingstoke, England, and Sydney, Australia. All the efforts were organized and coordinated through the main laboratory in Japan. Local technology centers, including the U.S. laboratory, also worked with local companies developing component parts.

HIRE LOCAL TALENT: BITTERSWEET GLOCALIZATION

Multinationals that have managed global operations for decades are realizing now that localizing operations is not the only piece of the puzzle. For decades, these global corporations have been sending staff from their home office, paying them a high premium of hefty salaries, housing stipends and hardship allowances to lure them abroad, often to developing countries, to run the local operations for the parent company. But in recent years, global corporations are feeling that the cost of sending expatriates abroad is too heavy a burden to bear, and the expatriates typically don't have the breadth of knowledge in a local market that the locals do. So there has been a shift in the way global corporations staff their overseas offices.

Sony is no exception. From the outset, Morita believed that to run overseas operations successfully, local talent had to be used. Presidents of Sony subsidiaries were hired locally and local management was actively promoted throughout the 1970s and 1980s. Morita believed that negotiations with local governments to construct new plants, for example, were better left in the hands of local management who understand both the accepted business protocols as well as the local language. Not only did this help Sony get a local perspective on how to manage globally, it also helped the company to become better integrated into the local communities. After all, the workers in Sony's factories lived in the towns and villages around the plants.

But hiring locally also meant one more challenge for Sony: coping with differences of management philosophy and culture. Take Harvey Schein, for example. He had shown promise as the ideal American manager for Sony, and had certainly delivered, building a solid management infrastructure and introducing the company to budget and cost control. But Schein was never able to modulate his abrasive American style, and had eventually worn down Morita's tolerance. It would be another 10 years before Sony would attempt to hire another American manager, and the candidate, Schein's protégé and eventual successor, Michael Schulhof, would pose a new challenge for Sony.

When Morita first met him, he was immediately drawn to Schulhof, a fellow physicist by training. On his frequent trips to Japan, Schulhof impressed Sony's scientists and technicians with the reach of his own technical understanding. Ibuka himself pronounced him a fascinating young man, and looked forward to talking shop with him. Morita and Ohga viewed Schulhof as the smartest of Schein's managerial team. He was ambitious and entrepreneurial, and he turned out to be masterly (precisely where Schein had been inept) at tuning into and accommodating the Japanese sensibility.

Just as the founders took Norio Ohga under their wing, Ohga and Morita quickly adopted Schulhof into the Sony family, and his career at Sony, like Ohga's own, was protected and privileged. When, in 1979, one of Schulhof's younger brothers was killed in a midair collision in a chartered plane, his father asked him to help with the family's greeting-card business. Morita showed patience and tenacity — just as he had done when the young Ohga insisted on pursuing his singing career before settling down with the company. "Look, I'm the eldest son also," he told Schulhof. "In Japan, we have obligations too. You go and help the family business as much as you want, but I won't let you leave Sony." So Sony installed a telephone line at the family firm and Schulhof worked there, all the while remaining a Sony employee for four years.

With Ohga, who later became president of Sony when Schulhof was head of U.S. operations, the friendship grew from their common passion for aviation. Schulhof used that very personal chemistry between the two to influence the company's behavior profoundly during the late 1980s and 1990s. Acting as Ohga's representative, Schulhof was a principal figure in Sony's acquisition of CBS Records in 1987 and, two years later, of Columbia TriStar Pictures. Subsequently, as CEO and chairman of all the American companies, he managed a US$15-billion piece of Sony's global business with a degree of authority never achieved by any foreigner before or since, at Sony or any other Japanese business organization.[5]

As close as Schulhof got to Morita and Ohga, the independent-mindedness of the American got the better of him. When Idei, Ohga's successor, became president in March 1995, Schulhof received a letter from Idei admonishing him to be a better team player. Over the years, Schulhof had made a lot of enemies within Sony. He was blamed by Teruo Tokunaka, then president and CEO of Sony Computer Entertainment, home of Sony's PlayStation, of trying to block the launch of the game console in the U.S. He also got in trouble for being disrespectful to Masaaki Morita. Schulhof had explained in a *New York Times* interview that he reported to no one but Norio Ohga. Morita phoned him angrily from Tokyo to let him know in no uncertain terms that he was expected to demonstrate appropriate respect for the executive chain of command, particularly where Masaaki Morita was concerned. It was clear to most observers that when Idei assumed leadership at Sony, Schulhof's days would be numbered. On December 4, 1995, Ohga informed Schulhof that his time was up. Whether Ohga wanted it that way, it was clear that within Sony Schulhof had many critics. As Ohga himself put it: "When you're running a business, you have no choice… Mickey's era was over. It was very hard because I had treated him like my younger brother. It hurt me. But if it was in Sony's interest, and I was certain it was, I had no choice."

Schulhof's resignation left Sony's U.S. operations without a president for a while. It highlighted yet another failed attempt by Sony to find an appropriate American manager who could both run the U.S. operations smoothly and juggle the delicate balance between the company's Japanese and American cultures.

GETTING THE HIRING FORMULA RIGHT

One of the biggest challenges any global company faces is finding appropriate talent abroad with both local market knowledge and cultural sensitivity, and a willingness to work well with the company's top management.

For Sony, this is an especially difficult challenge. Harvey Schein and Mickey Schuloff, former heads of Sony Corporation of America, in the 1950s and 1990s respectively, both joined Sony as prized local talent. They left amidst cultural and philosophical disagreements over management style with the top management in Tokyo. Peter Guber and Jon Peters, the duo who reigned over the Sony movie studios in the early 1990s, also left hastily when Tokyo headquarters finally had enough of their flamboyant and extravagent styles.

Knowledge and experience aside, good communication should be the most important quality to look for in local talent. After all, the foreign manager is the company's public face abroad, and the source of intelligence for headquarters on the market prospects and consumer behavior overseas. We can turn to Sony Music for an example of how bad communication strains the relationships between an overseas business unit and headquarters. In January 2003, Tommy Mottola, chief executive of Sony Music Entertainment, was forced out largely because of the way his management style clashed with his bosses. (Sony Music also needed a fresh face who could cut costs and navigate through the labyrinth of challenges facing the music industry today: declining CD sales, online piracy and strained relations with artists over contracts, to name a few.)

During his 14-year tenure with Sony Music, Mottola ran the music division as his personal fiefdom and did not include any top Sony executives in discussions about how the division was being run. He earned more than the company's top executives in Japan — as much as US$20 million some years — and spent lavishly on parties at his estates in Miami, the Hamptons or upstate New York. He rode an exclusive elevator to his office on the 32nd floor of Sony's Manhattan headquarters and refused to fly to Japan unless he was asked personally by Sony's chairman, Nobuyuki Idei.

But while Mottola enjoyed the high life of a music mogul, Sony's music business faltered. Domestic market shares has slipped almost 2 per cent since 1999, according to SoundScan, which tracks album sales. Mottola also failed to capitalize on the growth of urban music. Talented new artists, including the Grammy winner Alicia Keys and the singer Ashanti, were not always embraced at Sony and became superstars at other labels. The onslaught of free downloadable music online also hurt the music industry's profits; Sony Music was no exception.

For Sony, the combination of dwindling profits in the music industry as a whole and Mottola's overly independent management style meant that Sony Music needed a fresh start. His replacement, Andrew Lack, has no background in the music business, but his experience rebuilding the NBC News division and his close friendship with Howard Stringer, Sony's U.S. chief, make it more likely that he will fit better into Sony's corporate culture.[6]

JUGGLING PHILOSOPHIES: MORITA'S TAKE ON U.S. MANAGEMENT

The demise of Schein and Schulhof at Sony Corporation of America highlighted perhaps the biggest challenge Sony faced in coping with the global scale of its operations. Morita and

Ibuka knew that they had to go abroad and seek out new markets, and they were prepared to do so. They trained Japanese employees who spoke English and other languages to go out to find the potential business, establish the connections, and make the deals that would solidify Sony's international base. They even sought out talented local businessmen in the countries in which Sony operated and entrusted them to take care of the company's business abroad.

But Morita and Ibuka were perhaps ill-prepared to deal with the cultural clash that would be inevitable for any corporation extending beyond its home turf. In particular, Morita wrote extensively in his autobiography about the differences between American and Japanese management philosophies. As much as Morita tried to learn to understand the American ways, he had definite opinions and set ways of doing business, localization or not. He always chided American managers for their short-term outlook. In a book he published with Shintaro Ishihara, a conservative politician, in 1989, he recalled a chat with a money trader in New York: "I enquired how far ahead he looks. One week? 'No, no' came the reply. 'Ten minutes.' If Americans think only in terms of ten-minute action, while we Japanese think in ten-year terms, America assuredly faces gradual decline."

That was one of the major reasons Schein and Morita had clashed. Morita felt that the main goal of American management at Sony Corporation of America under Schein was profit. In Morita's view, profit didn't have to be so high because, in Japanese companies, he explained, shareholders do not clamor for immediate returns, preferring long-term growth and appreciation. Sony had to make a profit, but "we have to make a profit over the long haul", not just the short term. This meant that Sony had to keep investing in

"If you ask a
Japanese executive,
'What is your most
important responsibility?'
he will invariably say that
continued employment and
improving the livelihood of the
workers is at or near the top of
the list. In order to do that the
company must make a profit,
but making a profit will never
be at the top of the list."
— Akio Morita, founder

research and development, which can turn out to be a costly proposal. When Morita announced plans to open an extensive service center in Kansas City to establish a more complete customer-service network, he met challenge from Schein's managers over cost. "If you ask a Japanese executive, 'What is your most important responsibility?' he will invariably say that continued employment and improving the livelihood of the workers is at or near the top of the list. In order to do that the company must make a profit," Morita said. "But making a profit will never be at the top of the list."

EXTENDING THE SONY FAMILY

Despite the fact that Morita wanted a global company with local operations, he never strayed too far from the concept of Sony as a unified whole. Along with Ohga, he facilitated meetings between overseas subsidiaries and through the International Top Management meetings, and they often traveled to the subsidiaries themselves.

On the 25th anniversary of Sony America, Morita and his wife, Yoshiko, flew to the U.S. They arranged it so that they could have a picnic with the New York staff and could sit down to a meal with the three shifts at Sony's Dothan, Alabama, tape plant as well as the San Diego factory. On that trip, they also visited and dined with employees in Chicago and Los Angeles. As Morita recalled it in his autobiography, "It was a very satisfying thing for me, and I think they were pleased to see me and my wife. It was not just part of my job; I like those people. They are family."

Morita and Ohga's goal internationally was to establish an identity for Sony that extended beyond borders and they stuck religiously to Sony's fundamental principles. Sony's top management met regularly with employees in Japan and abroad, and spoke of the Sony philosophy as often as possible. They enjoyed being on close terms with employees and their families worldwide. When the company opened its factory in the United Kingdom, it took the plant managers and engineers to Tokyo and let them work with the workers there. It gave them Sony jackets and ate with them in Sony's one-class cafeteria. This way, Morita said, he hoped they got to understand that people should not be treated differently. And this way, Morita felt, these British managers would understand and appreciate the culture of their employer.

Sony always stationed some of its Japanese executives at overseas operations. As one Japanese overseas employee put it recently, "We bring Sony culture to the table [wherever we are]. After all, wherever Sony is, the people who work for Sony are part of the family." Among Sony lifers are some of the company's most senior executives who spent considerable time working outside Japan. For example, Kenji Tamiya worked in the United States and South America for 20 years. Morita led by example. "It struck me that if we were going to be successful as a company in the giant American market, we would have to do more than establish our company on

"We bring Sony culture to the table [wherever we are]. After all, wherever Sony is, the people who work for Sony are part of the family." — Sony overseas employee

American soil. I would have to move my family to the United States and experience the life of an American," Morita wrote later. In 1963, not long after Sony laid down the foundation stones of its U.S. operations, Morita took his wife and children to the U.S. to live. Their time in the U.S., though cut short by the unexpected death of Morita's father, was crucial to Morita's understanding of American business practices and commonly accepted behavior. But in his short stay and in subsequent visits on behalf of the company, he made some very influential American friends, including former Secretary of State Henry Kissinger.

ESTABLISH CORPORATE GOVERNANCE

Even with Morita's sometime discomfort with American management philosophies, he accepted and learned how to run a business the American way. In the late 1980s, he looked at Sony's globalization and realized that the task wasn't complete. He invited Schulhof and Jakob Schmuckli, who headed Sony Europe at the time, to join Sony Group's Board of Directors in June 1989. In Japan, then and now, it was incredibly rare for a company to have non-Japanese employees from their overseas subsidiaries join the board of the parent company, though many executives do sit on the boards of listed subsidiaries. For example, the current chairman of Sony Corporation of America, Sir Howard Stringer, sits on the board of Sony Europe.

The aim of Morita and Ohga in appointing them to the board was to promote key international management and to demonstrate to other non-Japanese management that they were just as important to Sony as their Japanese counterparts. This would form the next step in the globalization of Sony's personnel strategy.

In the years after, Sony would appoint other non-Japanese to its board of directors, including Peter Peterson, who was the chairman of the Blackstone Group. Peterson had known Morita for more than three decades. They got to know each other while serving together on the Pan American International Advisory Committee. When Sony was named in a collective antitrust suit brought by an American television manufacturer, Emerson, for dumping televisions into the American market in 1970, Morita paid Peterson a call. Peterson, at the time, was President Richard Nixon's assistant on international economic affairs. Although Peterson was not in a position to influence the suit, he did help Morita arrange a meeting at the White House with Nixon and other Japanese CEOs to discuss trade issues. Later, when Peterson had left the government to head Lehman Brothers, Morita asked him for guidance in designing an executive compensation plan, something unheard of in Japan at that time. In 1988 and 1989, the private investment bank Peterson had founded in 1985, the Blackstone Group, played a central role in Sony's acquisition of CBS Records and Columbia Pictures. In 1992, he accepted Morita's invitation to become the first American not employed by Sony to sit on the Sony board. Peterson was also the one who brought John Calley on board with Sony Pictures Entertainment in the mid 1990s after losses at the Sony studios had prompted a serious management shake-up. (Now, the Sony board has diversified even more. At the time of writing, of the 11 members of the Board of Directors, three are outside directors.)

GLOBAL STRATEGY OF CONVERGENCE

Sony's efforts to build a global empire are clear. Among the Japanese companies able to do such a thing, Sony has probably been one of the more successful. Still, some critics have described Sony as unmistakably still a Japanese company at core. Despite collaborations with its R&D teams, its marketing people and its employees, the direction of the company is still almost entirely dictated from the Tokyo headquarters.

Sony's strategic vision for the 21st century is to become the global leader in the entertainment industry by using its unique combination of hardware and software capabilities. Because of the unique importance of the U.S. as a market, as a global center in development and manufacturing as well as the critical platform for its emerging software strategy, synchronizing the U.S. operations with those the parent company has become even more crucial. One of the challenges is to achieve a subtle balance of influence between the product divisions and the U.S. operations. The second major challenge is the extent to which the various operations within the U.S. should be integrated. What role should Sony

Corporation of America play in coordinating all of this? Should its role be expanded? And the third challenge, and a very real one today, is how to achieve integration between the company's software and hardware businesses. Hardware development resided largely in Japan, whereas the center for software development was in the U.S. How much and how fast should management try to integrate across oceans and continents?

Overall, globalization has been an important strategic agenda for Sony. And for the most part, Sony has developed a brand name for itself that allows it to hire good staff and sell good products. Now, its challenge is to evaluate how all the pieces of its global picture will fit together to maximize its resources. That is a formidable challenge, and one that perhaps only Sony, with its history of global vision, could best take on.

SONY'S RECIPES FOR SUCCESS

• *Dare to take risks:* Who says a small Japanese upstart can't become a global giant? Determination and the courage to venture beyond home boundaries is the first step in any internationalization strategy.

• *Think global, act local:* A principle that is now common to many major enterprises, it is a crucial piece of any global strategy. To be able to market your products to other countries, you have to develop a keen understanding of the local culture, the consumers' behavior and needs, and knowledge of all local business processes including manufacturing, marketing and distribution.

- *Seize every opportunity*: Don't overlook the smaller or less-developed markets. They could be a gold-mine for business opportunities. They may be riskier, more uncertain, but measured risks often reap rewards.

- *Innovate across borders, communicate across borders*: Part of the challenge of running a global company is making the different units around the world speak to one another. It is vital to communicate frequently and clearly so that the company can leverage the talent it has in different countries to formulate the best strategies for the company. This is one of the greatest benefits of going global — having the ability to draw upon talents and good ideas around the world to make the best products and brainstorm the best business strategies.

- *Hire local talent*: Not only does this save corporations the hefty compensation packages often required to send employees abroad, hiring local management talent also immediately gives you the knowledge base and understanding of local culture that an expatriate executive might take months or years to learn. In a sense it is killing two birds with one stone: not only can it give the company a different perspective on how to manage globally, it can also lead to a greater acceptance of the company by local communities.

NOTES

1.	Morita et al, *Made In Japan: Akio Morita and Sony*, op. cit.

2.	Nathan, *Sony: The Private Life*, op. cit.

3.	Michael Y. Yoshino and Thomas W. Malnight, "Sony Corporation: Globalization", *Harvard Business Review*, October 15, 1990.

4. *Genryu*, Sony Corporation of America, 1996.

5. Gene Bylinsky, "Where Japan Will Strike Next?", *Fortune*,
    September 25, 1989, p.42.

6. Laura M. Holson and Bill Carter, "NBC President to Take
    Over at Sony Music", *The New York Times*, January 11,
    2003.

Three

STAY AHEAD: FEEDING THE INNOVATIVE ENGINE

There was a time when anything shipped abroad and marked "Made In Japan" was associated with paper umbrellas, kimonos, toys and cheap trinkets. Sony played a key role in changing that stereotype and helped establish Japan's reputation for innovation by defying a tradition of copying the products of others. This drive to be original gave birth to some of Sony's most popular consumer products, such as the extremely successful Trinitron color television, Sony Walkmans, video camcorders and now MP3 players. This chapter seeks to capture this innovative spirit to show how Sony emerged from the crowd of nameless Asian electronics companies to become a global brand.

I n the late 1950s, a reporter for a leading Japanese weekly described Sony as a corporate guinea pig, implying that the company played the sacrificial lamb to the industry. Once the work tested by the "guinea pig" is deemed feasible, the reporter wrote, large corporations jump on it and make it their own and better. When Ibuka and his engineers heard the metaphor, they didn't take it as a kind description (and it probably wasn't meant to be). Ibuka resented the reporter's condescension. But in later years, he hailed this metaphor as a symbol of Sony's innovative spirit. "By taking this guinea pig approach to products, there is always something new to challenge," he said.[1]

The Gold Guinea pig — Courtesy of Sony Corporation

It is no surprise that people have looked at Sony as the guinea pig, pioneer, innovator. This is the kind of company that Ibuka had envisioned when he wrote the founding prospectus for Sony Corporation in 1946. He wanted a corporate environment that would nurture engineers and allow them to stretch their imagination. He wanted a company that broke ranks from the copycat image that tarnished the reputation of Japanese manufacturers at the time. It was an important and challenging goal Ibuka tried to set for his fledgling company of eight employees, but one that was undoubtedly crucial to the success of Sony.

"By taking this guinea pig approach to products, there is always something new to challenge." — Masaru Ibuka, founder

In the years leading up to the Second World War, the tag "Made In Japan" meant cheap imitations to the rest of the world, similar to the way many people now associate cheap toys and low-end electronics manufacturing with Japan's Southeast Asian neighbors and China. Pre-war Japan was a manufacturing hub for American and European companies; its comparatively low wages made it an attractive place to subcontract basic manufacturing processes. Innovation was hardly encouraged — the money was made from mass-producing designs from Western companies cheaply and reselling them abroad. This was the stereotype that Ibuka and Morita wanted desperately to change.

Ibuka wanted to create useful devices for Japanese consumers — and later, at Morita's urging, for consumers everywhere in the world. The concepts of creation and innovation are therefore the core of what Sony represents.[2] It is that very drive to disprove this copycat image that motivated Sony engineers to take risks, giving birth to some of Sony' most popular consumer products, such as the Walkman in 1979, the extremely successful Trinitron color television in 1967 and, in this millennium, the Clié handheld organizer.

In the business world, it is simple to choose to be a follower, to look at what others are doing and copy and refine it. After all, the risks that come with being an industry leader are often too great financially for some companies to bear. But the rewards, many industry leaders would tell you, are far greater. Sony is fortunate that it had founders who shared that vision of innovation, and a team of engineers ready to live out that dream, understanding that it was a case of invent or perish in post-war Japan. When Sony started out, it had neither an established reputation nor the business experience of seasoned managers to push it ahead. So the engineers relied heavily on each other's minds and imaginations.

Ibuka was the principal driver behind Sony's innovative direction, the inspiration behind Sony's first projects. When he received an award from the emperor commending him for his contributions in innovation and technology, Sony employees presented him with a custom-made gold guinea pig as a gift, which Ibuka placed on his desk as a reminder every day of his vision for the company. Ibuka's vision, together with Morita's marketing genius (which will be discussed in a later chapter), pulled Sony products out from a pool of nameless Asian brands to become a common and popular sight in households around the globe.

THE FATHER OF SONY INNOVATION

"Purpose of incorporation: creating an ideal workplace, free, dynamic, and joyous, where dedicated engineers will be able to realize their craft and skills at the highest possible level."

Sony's Founding Prospectus

Ibuka had a great gift of foreseeing product applications for new technologies and inspiring his engineers to stretch themselves in achieving the goals he set. Sony engineers who knew Ibuka worship his memory and characterize their years of working with him as the most creative and gratifying period of their careers. Technology was his lifelong passion. As a second-grader in Tokyo, Ibuka was given an Erector Set, which, in his own words, taught him "the excitement of putting things together". In high school, he became an avid ham-radio operator, a hobby he enjoyed all his life.

A mechanical engineering student by training, Ibuka made his first invention in college. He created something he called a "light telephone", which used high-frequency sound waves to control the intensity of a light. Ibuka succeeded in using the device to "send a visible signal as far as a mile and half". The success of this experiment earned him a reputation as "Ibuka, the student inventor". Subsequently he adapted the same technology to create a product he called "dancing neon", which he patented in his own name. The product was submitted to the Paris World Fair in 1933, and won the Gold Prize for invention. The headline in a Tokyo newspaper read: "Basking in the light of international recognition: a genius inventor."

But no one ever said that promising innovators always gets the recognition they deserve. In the year Ibuka won the World Fair's Gold Prize, he took an employment exam at Shibaura Electric Company (now known as Toshiba Corp.) and failed. Fortunately, entrepreneur Taiji Uemura had heard about Ibuka's inventiveness and invited him to join his company, Photo-chemical Laboratories (PCL). Recognizing that Ibuka was not a person to be managed, Uemura gave his new employee the freedom to follow his own research interests. By 1936, with Japanese military aggression expanding in Asia, Ibuka became interested in ways of combining electrical and mechanical engineering to create weapons applications, including a vessel-location system. Uemura helped Ibuka to found Japan Measuring Instruments Co., which would become a weapons manufacturer during the Second World War. When Japan announced its defeat in 1945, Ibuka realized that his company would not be equipped to take advantage of the peacetime market, so he decided to leave. Taking seven engineers with him, Ibuka moved into the Shirokiya Department Store, the first home of what would later become Sony Corporation.

INNOVATIVE FROM THE HEART

"Everything starts from the heart. It is impossible to conceive a product without heart. By satisfying people's hearts, science gains value in itself."
Masaru Ibuka, founder [3]

Some say that great entrepreneurs are endowed with the capacity to perceive sharply things that are invisible to ordinary eyes. They possess an innate gift, one that cannot be taught or learned. To a certain extent, this may be true; but, Sony designers and engineers believe, the spirit of innovation comes very much from the heart. In the opening lines of Sony's founding prospectus, Ibuka declares that his company will be designed by and for engineers: "My first and primary objective was establishing a stable workplace where engineers could work to their hearts' content in full consciousness of their joy in technology and their social obligation."

From the color of the Walkman shell to the shape of each key on the highly stylized VAIO laptop computer, Sony gives its engineers the room and time to labor over the details that distinguish Sony's products from others. Sony has dedicated design centers around the world that worry solely about the look of a product, the shades of color, the shape, the placement of keys and buttons. It also has separate research and development centers that focus on a specific business segment, such as wireless or audio or visual products.

Although most development projects are largely dictated from the top executives, many engineers in Sony's design and product-development centers say they also quietly work on inventions of their own that could one day become part of the Sony product line. In fact, one of the company's most well-known products, the Walkman, was, so they say, the result of an accidental discovery by Sony engineers. One version of the story recounts a visit by Akio Morita to the product-development center where he stumbled on an engineer who was testing a prototype for what would become the Walkman. By this time, Sony's transistor radios and tape recorders were becoming popular. The engineer thought that consumers might want to have a smaller, portable version of the tape recorder. Morita thought the engineer had a good idea that could turn into an interesting product, and that was the beginning of the Sony Walkman.

Sony Walkman — Courtesy of Sony Corporation

There are, however, several other versions of how the Walkman came to be, one of which Morita himself retells in his autobiography. But the point of retelling this story is to illustrate a Sony culture that encourages engineers to think outside the box. Describing Sony's innovative spirit is like describing the family values that make up its corporate culture. Both share a similar foundation of values about risk-taking and trust between employees and management.

HOW SONY FOUND THE TAPE-CORDER

From the outset, Ibuka had always wanted to produce something that would directly benefit the general public, who he considered to be quite different from the government and other institutional customers. But it was not just any product that Ibuka wanted. Radios had already been introduced into the Japanese markets by the larger conglomerates. Morita was then also looking, purely from a business point of view, for a product with which Sony could expand its sales channels. It was then that the wire recorder attracted the attention of the co-founders.

Wire recorders had existed in Japan since the pre-war period, but the quality of sound was not ideal. Ibuka and his colleagues decided to enter the wire recorder market, setting an ambitious goal of improving the sound quality of the device. But, given the material shortages existing in war-devastated Japan, wires could not be produced easily, and the amount of wire needed to produce the recorders seemed like a rather unreasonable request. Without wires, nothing could be done. The wire recorder itself also posed many technical problems. It would be extremely difficult to repair a broken wire. The recording head would wear quickly. Long recordings would be impossible. Moreover, recording noise would make it even less attractive. So, with all these barriers, Sony gave up the wire recorder business.

While still working hard on the wire recorder, Sony heard of a machine that could reproduce sound on tape. At that time, Ibuka and Morita were frequent visitors to the American Occupation Forces headquarters. One day, an official showed them a tape recorder — the sound was markedly better than that from a wire recorder and made a lasting impression on them. "This is the consumer product we must produce," Ibuka said to Morita after seeing the tape recorder. "It has great potential. Let's do it with tape." The first prototype of the Tape-corder was completed in September 1949. And the first marketable tape recorder by Sony was made available in 1950.

TRIAL AND ERROR

There is no invention that is perfect from the beginning. Successful devices all have their story of failures, refinements and tweaking before becoming ideal models. Failures inevitably happen in the development process. How can they not? When you innovate, you are creating something new and you'll never know if an invention is a winning product unless you have tried and tested it repeatedly.

Some failures, however, are more serious than others but, as discussed earlier, the idea that everyone works as a team at Sony allows employees the leeway to take bigger risks in their trials, especially when the person taking the plunge is the founder himself. On his 84th birthday, when Ibuka was asked to name his proudest moment in Sony history, he responded, "Trinitron". Sony's color-television picture tube is one of its most valuable assets: at the end of 1998, 180 million Trinitron picture tubes had been sold worldwide. The first 12-inch Trinitron was released in 1968, but the development process, perhaps one of Sony's most trying projects, began years before that, in 1961.

It may seem odd to invoke a failure to tell a story about success, but there is probably no better way to look at Sony's innovative spirit than through one of its biggest blunders and one of Ibuka's pet projects: the Chromatron Tube Project.

Color television had been available in America since the mid fifties, but the technology was not the most refined. The default technology had been developed by Radio Corporation of America (RCA), the market leader at the time. RCA's device comprised three separate electron guns, one for each primary color, which fired their beams at a focusing mechanism called a shadow mask, which then converged them on their way to the picture screen. For complex technical reasons, radiance was compromised as the beams passed through the shadow mask and this resulted in a darkened screen image with muddied resolution. The lackluster picture and premium pricing discouraged sales, but there was no question in anyone's mind that if the resolution were refined, the potential market for color television would be tremendous.

By 1961, Sony had fallen seriously behind the competition and still the company seemed to have no plans for entering the color-television market. Dealers were beginning to ask when they could expect Sony's color entry. There was pressure from the sales division to purchase a ready-made system and market it as a Sony product. Ibuka refused. That would run against the very pioneering spirit that made Sony known to the international market, and relegate Sony to the ranks of other copycat manufacturers, a reputation that Ibuka vowed to avoid.

At a trade show in March that year, Ibuka and Morita found the technology that they were looking for — a Chromatron, a color tube used by the U.S. military that emitted sharp, bright images. Sony eagerly bought the technology, not knowing that it would never succeed in mass-producing it. For two years, Sony's Chromatron team labored to develop a commercial prototype and a process technology for mass production. Part of the trick of this one-electron gun device was controlling the focus and acceleration of the electron beam at high voltage, but that was only a sliver of what turned out to be a production nightmare. By September 1964, three years after Sony bought the Chromatron technology, a prototype with a 17-inch screen was ready, but mass-production problems had not been eliminated and test runs were not promising.

Ibuka alone was confident, insisting that the product would succeed. He displayed the product in the Sony showroom, creating market excitement and pressure for its success. But mass-production problems were never solved. Out of 1,000 picture tubes, only two or three were usable. Others suffered from "color variance", with faces going green at the outer edges and greens merging sickeningly into reds. Ibuka refused to give up. He made the project the company's top priority, putting a dedicated team of 150 people to work on Chromatron. The machines sold in Japan at a retail price of ¥198,000 (US$550), but each set cost over ¥400,000 to produce. Eventually, 13,000 sets were sold at a huge loss to the company. In November 1966, Iwama told one of his colleagues that the company was "close to ruin", and that Chromatron would have to be abandoned by the end of the year if production yields could not be improved.

Ibuka perhaps realized the futility of the Chromatron project and decided in 1966, after five years of work on the technology, that he personally would lead a team to search for an alternative. Despite sentiments within the company that it should adopt RCA's shadow-mask system, Ibuka was determined to find his own way into the color-television market. He was unwilling to allow five years of work to end with imitation. As Morita struggled to calm Sony dealers waiting anxiously for the company to produce a color television that could compete with rival models, he was also governed by his respect for Ibuka. To finance the additional R&D costs, he secured a loan from Japan Development Bank, Sony's first development loan, of ¥650 million (roughly US$2 million at the time) at 6.5 per cent interest. (The eventual success of Trinitron, then still a long way off, would enable the company to repay the loan in three years.)

The engineers on Ibuka's team began exploring different approaches to color, but little progress was made. Then one day, one of the engineers, Susumu Yoshida, wondered aloud about what might happen if the three cathodes were used to generate three electron beams from a single gun. Although skeptical, the engineers tried it. And to their surprise, they produced a screen image in color, blurred but bright, unaccountably bright.

In the months that followed, the Sony engineers refined and tested, realizing that they might have finally found their solution to color television. In April 1968, some seven years after Sony first embarked on its quest to find its own color-television technology, Trinitron finally came to life.

Was it worth jeopardizing the company's entire financial position for a dream that may or may not be realized? Many say the Chromatron project crippled Sony financially at the time. But without embarking on the doomed project, Sony's engineers would not have discovered that they could combine the shadow-mask system with Chromatron's one-tube technology to make today's Trinitron televisions.

Trial and error is part of technological innovation. Without taking risks with Chromatron, the success that eventually followed might never have been achieved.

DON'T GIVE UP EASILY

An integral part of the innovative spirit is trial and error. Test and refine. Along the way there are bound to be failures but you must persist, even if you have to shelve the idea for a few years. Inventions such as the Sony Trinitron or the VAIO computer wouldn't have been possible if the engineers at Sony had simply given up after two or three failures. (In the case of personal computers, it would be another decade before Sony tried to enter the PC market again.) The flip side of persistence, however, is losing sight of when to let go. Sometimes you can be persistent but never find a solution that could make your product marketable. In the end, you run the risk of draining your company's financial resources and lowering morale within the company.

DO YOUR OWN WORK. DON'T COPY. LEAD

At the Sony product museum at the company's headquarters in Tokyo, a sign on the wall sums up Sony's innovative spirit concisely and aptly: "Never imitate. Create from the heart. Look into the future for ideas."

As mentioned earlier, Sony's first years were spent dispelling an image the West had of Japanese manufacturers as cheap imitators who made simplified copies of what were believed to be superior Western devices. Sony's Tape-corder, its pocket-size transistor radio, Walkman and compact discs have certainly set the record straight that Sony is a pioneer, not a copycat.

But how do you keep this innovative machine revved up?

Ibuka, the dreamer and inventor, would answer: at all costs. As exemplified by the Chromatron failure, Ibuka was adamant that the devices that rolled out of the company's manufacturing plants were designed and developed by his own team of engineers, especially for the comfort and convenience of the consumers that Sony serves.

> "Never imitate. Create from the heart. Look into the future for ideas." — Sign in Sony Museum

The same determination and stubbornness also gave birth to the Walkman, the signature of Sony's success in innovation. When Morita decided that Sony should make a small portable audio-tape player, the engineers summoned to undertake the project objected. They doubted, as did the marketing executives, that consumers would want such a small tape player that, at the time, didn't have a recording function. But of course, as it turned out, the Walkman was a great success. The Walkman now comes in all sorts of models — more than 80 in total that are water-proof, sports, sand-proof models suited to satisfy consumers with different needs. No amount of marketing research could have told Sony that people would want a lightweight, portable tape player that was the Walkman. It just wasn't an option that consumers fathomed would even be possible. And yet this lightweight box has changed the listening habits of literally millions of people all around the world.

But while Sony does strive to be a pioneer in its industry, it isn't always the first to come up with the technology, as we saw with its attempts to make color television, and the first successful Sony VAIO computer wasn't introduced until 1997, more than two decades after the first personal computers were available on the consumer market.

Leading Japanese and American experts have different theories about Japanese creativity, but both sides agree on one point: Americans tend to excel at breakthrough research, while Japanese are better at adapting ideas and technologies to create new products and markets. Some scholars have explained it like this: the Japanese are better at "adaptive creativity", the art of refining ideas within the framework of new theories. This systematic approach is more suitable for process innovations and complex systems research, such as factory automation software or high-definition television, both of which require the kind of continuity and teamwork that is intrinsic to companies like Sony.[4]

Adaptive creativity is a way of responding creatively to breakthroughs. For example, Sony sometimes takes existing technology, even its own ideas such as miniaturization or multiple use, and combines it with other ideas to develop new products.

These refinements have brought about distinctly Sony innovations. Look at the compact disk, which Sony developed jointly with Dutch electronics giant, Philips Electronics. Or the PlayStation, which at the time was the first to allow buyers to play both cartridge and compact-disc games. Or the Sony Handycam, the first 8mm video camera available on the market. These creations helped Sony earn licensing fees in addition to product sales that have supported the company's bottom line. But as technologies become more standardized and accessible to others, it is no longer purely about being technologically competitive, but whether you can make others accept your technology as the standard. That is perhaps one of the greatest challenges Sony faces, and one where it has tasted failure, particularly in the Betamax debacle.

Some critics say that Sony hasn't been as successful in recent years in keeping ahead of its competitors in either technological sophistication or in appealing to a mass audience — the two things on which it had built its reputation. But the electronics industry is a tug-of-war — you gain some ground, but you lose some elsewhere. You have to be flexible and ready to adjust when necessary. In some respects, Sony, taking extreme pride in its superior technology, can be stubborn about budging, analysts say — and sometimes to its detriment.

DON'T JUST STOP AT ONE THING. REINVENT AND REFINE

In recent years, the electronics market from which Sony derives the majority of its revenues has become a cut-throat industry, with consumers who are fickle and easily lured by newer, fancier, more sophisticated gadgets. The race to succeed is no longer a race to see who has the better technology, but to see who can reinvent themselves the fastest and satisfy the appetite and curiosity of gadget-hungry consumers.

In a market where technology is no longer the single differentiating factor, details make all the difference. Sony's core competence of miniaturization, which we will touch on later in the chapter, is an excellent example of how the company keeps reinventing and refining its gadgets to suit the needs of consumers, all the while staying ahead of its competitors. Or take the evolution of Sony's tape recorder. From the moment the first machine was made, and before it even hit the market, Sony's engineers were already back at the design table, refining and tweaking the original blueprints to get better sound and better quality tapes to the consumers. The first paper tapes for Sony's Tape-corder weren't of good quality. Ibuka said at the time said the quality was so bad you could hardly hear anyone say "moshi-moshi", the Japanese telephone greeting. The engineers at Sony kept refining the tape, eventually using plastic as the main material. And the testament to all the effort the company put into refining its recording tape came in November 1965, when IBM chose Sony's magnetic recording tape for data storage on its computers.

The close attention to appearance as well as the quality of the product is not just a natural evolution at a company already bursting with creativity, but an absolute necessity in order for it to retain its market share. In recent years, Sony has found itself in an increasingly crowded field of makers of low-cost, but high-quality electronics — all determined to build global brands like Sony's. Korea's Samsung Electronics Co., for example, is investing heavily in product development and marketing in a bid to challenge Sony in big markets like the U.S. The rivals have an advantage in that there are increasing numbers of standard technologies that they can buy, helping to level the playing field and allow them to bring products to market quickly. These new rivals from China, South Korea and the U.S. are attacking Sony's product strongholds in audio and visual equipment, and new technologies are erasing

Sony's technological advantage in key areas such as disks for data storage.

Now that the core underlying technology is widely and readily available to everyone, Sony tries to differentiate its products by pushing out new shapes, colors, sizes and combinations of features before its competitors; hence Sony's miniaturization and multiple-purpose strategies — a case of think big, make small.

THINK BIG, MAKE SMALL

Miniaturization and compactness have always appealed to the Japanese. Fans fold. Art rolls into neat scrolls. Screens that can artistically depict an entire city can be folded and tucked neatly away, or set up to delight, entertain and educate or merely to divide a room. The appeal of such things is perhaps obvious in a society with a dense population and an extreme shortage of living space. When Sony's transistor radios first became an established product, Ibuka and Morita set their hearts on making the radio better, smaller — pocketable. The goal was daunting. Sony's dealers in the U.S. and some of its engineers balked at the idea of miniaturizing the transistor radio. They didn't see a demand in a country like the U.S., where everything is monumental compared to Japan: houses are big; cars are wide; the land is so vast. Why would Americans want such a small device? (In fact, the Americans who licensed transistor technology to Sony never understood that the technology could be used to make radios. They told Sony's founders that the transistor technology was good only for use in hearing aids.)

But Ibuka and Morita were determined to make it work. Measuring 112 by 71 by 32 mm, and using six transistors for better reception and output, the pocketable radio, TR-63, made its first appearance in 1957. With the advent of the TR-63, the radio was set free from its position in the home and transformed into a personal effect. No longer part of the furniture, it would become a convenient aid to everyday living, which could be taken out of the house and listened to while walking, driving a car, or doing almost anything. At US$39.95, the TR-63 was introduced at Christmas time in the United States. Shipments could not keep up with the year-end demand, and a Japan Airlines plane had to be chartered to air-freight a large consignment.

TR-63 Transistor Radio — Courtesy of Sony Corporation

Ibuka and his engineers would later apply the same miniaturization principle to Sony's Trinitron television sets, and meet the same kind of resistance within the corporation once again.

In the last half a century, Sony has brought us even thinner and smaller products such as the 80 different versions of

Walkman, and the newest generation of Sony's digital cameras, Cybercam, which fits right in the back pocket of a pair of jeans.

Camcorders, for example, used tapes that fit right into your video tape player, but Sony's 8mm tape Handycam changed the way people thought about recording devices. When in April 1985 Sony declared its intention to produce video equipment in 8mm tape format, the reaction in the trade was one of hopeful surprise mixed with instant skepticism. Who, it was asked with a fair degree of unanimity, needs a third video format incompatible not just with the prevailing standard, VHS, but also with Sony's own Betamax? Radical miniaturization of this sort is the crux of Sony's innovation. At a time when all video design aspired to smallness and lightness, Betamax and VHS equipment — both using bulky cassettes with half-inch tape — were approaching their limits of possible miniaturization. Further reduction in weight and size of video gear would mean a new and inherently more compact tape format, and the 8mm cassettes opened up new possibilities here.

Sony's first product in the new format was a camera-recorder combination — an item where lightness and smallness counted as primary virtues. Weighing just five pounds, the Model CCD-8 "camcorder" was a truly agile tool for making one's own videos, yielding pictures of uncommon sharpness, with 300 lines of horizontal resolution. It featured an electronic viewfinder for instant playback, minimal power consumption of 6.6 watts for long battery life, and sold for US$1,695. And then in June that same year, Sony came out with a better model, called the Mini-8, a camcorder that weighed under two pounds, provided quality images and, with its companion videocassette recorder-player, sold for $1,800.

THINK OUTSIDE THE BOX

At Sony, the buzzwords among engineers go something like this: "something different, something new". It is this willingness to think outside the norm that brings consumers Sony innovation, from PlayStation to Airboard tablet television to a Clié handheld organizer with a digital camera and an MP3 player.

In a way, this Sony quality follows the logic of adaptive creativity. In recent years, Sony has, at times, been something of a latecomer into some consumer-device markets such as the handheld organizer, the personal computer and the game-console businesses. Yet, in each one of these product markets, it has been able to make an immediate impact, capture a chunk of the market share and, sometimes, even become the dominant player in the market. The Sony approach of making "something different, something new" has taken on a new spin — taking what exists in the market and recreating a product that gives new meaning to its purpose.

Take the Airboard, for example. The idea behind its creation is allowing consumers to have a portable, flat-screen that doubles as both a television and a computer so that consumers can take it anywhere in the house and be able to watch television and surf online. Computers as consumers know them today are typically big white boxes that sit on a desk in a company cubicle. Workers use them for word processing, email, surfing the Internet or making calculations on spreadsheets. At home, computers are confined largely to the study, where people may work on projects they bring home from school or the office. If they want to watch television, people go to the living room or the den and turn on their television sets. They generally have to move from one room to another in order to either watch television or use the computer. The Airboard idea is to be able to combine both functions and make the device mobile. If you're in the kitchen, you can bring the Airboard to the kitchen and watch television or surf the Internet there. Or if you're in your bedroom, you can take the Airboard there. Rather than being wired to a computer in a fixed location, the Airboard allows consumers to be mobile within their own homes. Right now, though, Sony recognizes that Airboard may not be a concept that consumers fully appreciate. So far, sales of the Airboard have not lived up to expectations, Sony officials say, but they are hoping that, with Microsoft reintroducing a slate computer, the concept will become more popular.

Once again, it may seem odd to use a less-than-successful Sony product — Airboard — to illustrate the strength of Sony's ability to think outside the box. But, to echo an earlier point, without the mistakes success may not be realized. A more powerful and frequently cited example of Sony thinking outside the box and succeeding is the PlayStation game console, a project that once met with vehement opposition from Sony engineers and executives, but is now one of the company's most profitable divisions.

Despite opposition, PlayStation's inventor, Ken Kutaragi, worked tirelessly to pitch his idea of making computer-game consoles that could support software for high-quality three-dimensional computer graphics and, in the end, his vocal promotion of the project was heard. (With PlayStation® 2,

Kutaragi created a game console that would double as a DVD player. It also had an adapter that could connect the machine to broadband Internet. The brilliance of PlayStation 2 is that it attempted to revolutionize the idea of what a game console should do for a consumer. The PlayStation story will unfold in greater detail in a later chapter.)

SIDEBAR ON SONY'S FORAY INTO COMPUTERS

VAIO C1 laptop — Courtesy of Sony Corporation

Sony's first computer-related product was the SOBAX, a desktop calculator first introduced in 1967. But Sony soon withdrew from this market in 1972 after a heated price war drove profit margins to a bare minimum. In the early 1970s, Intel Corp.'s development of the microprocessor and the introduction of personal computers set the world off on a steady course toward computerization. At the time, Sony's management decided that since the company's core electronics business focused on audio and visual equipment for the masses, its R&D efforts in the computer field were to be minimal.

Kazuo Iwama, who became president in 1976, had a gut feeling that companies that did not understand computers would not survive the 1990s. PCs made their first appearance in 1975, and in 1978 Toshiba launched the first Japanese-language word processor. Iwama supervised the gradual development of computers at Sony. At the end of the 1970s, a team led by Yoshiro Kato and Kenji Hori began the development of computer-related products in the office automation (OA) and microcomputer (MC) fields. Sony's efforts in office automation eventually led to the introduction of an English-language word processor and a portable typewriter that featured a liquid crystal display. In the home PC field, Sony introduced the "HIT BIT" model, which at the time conformed to the Microsoft-led MSX standard, commercialized in November 1983.

Sony always envisioned that somehow these computer products would converge with the company's traditional focus in the video and audio fields. When Norio Ohga became president in 1985, he poured a lot of effort into expanding this computer link with the audio and video fields. Unfortunately, Sony was never able to establish a presence in this market, despite continuous efforts by the development team. Sony's computer-related products launched in the 1980s were eventually phased out or discontinued due to a lack of interest in the market.

When Sony made its final foray into the PC business in the mid 1990s, it was already way behind its competitors. But because the Sony VAIO computer was a latecomer, it was able to exploit the increasing popularity of digital music and video-taping to produce a computer that had both music and video-editing capacities. Sony resisted the white-box-plus-monitor mode and decided that the VAIO computer was going to be something different, appealing to a consumer's imagination.

Sony's VAIO personal computer and Clié handheld organizer also follow the same principle of changing the way the consumer thinks about the purpose of a particular device. Entering late into the PC market, Sony wanted to make a computer that would challenge the traditional concepts of what a computer does. Introduced in 1997, the VAIO (its full name being "video and audio integrated operation") encapsulates the idea of the desktop computer as being something more than a workstation. It is a machine that enables consumers to play music, manipulate graphics and photographs, watch movies and enjoy entertainment in general. The Clié follows a similar logic. Introduced in 2000, it sets out to change consumers' perceptions of what a handheld organizer should do. Instead of just being a substitute for an address book and diary, the latest models of the Clié have built-in digital cameras, built-in keyboards and the capability to download music and movie trailers. The idea, Sony executives say, is to create a handheld that would serve as a portable entertainment center rather than just a simple device to record addresses, phone numbers and appointments.

THE VAIO CUBE PHILOSOPHY

To enter a market as a latecomer and succeed in winning a sizeable market share is an impressive feat. In Japan, VAIO computer products as a whole claim close to half of the market share for personal computers. Its sleek, silvery purple design and its audio- and video-editing software have lured technophiles to gravitate toward the Sony VAIO over other branded personal computers.

But the journey to design the VAIO computer was not an easy one, particularly because Sony had failed twice before in its attempts to enter the personal computer marketplace. To inspire engineers, Sony executives came up with a philosophy for VAIO, a summation of what the computer would stand for. Today, the six-word philosophy is made into a design the shape of a cube, and placed in front of every VAIO engineer and designer's work space, encouraging them to continue to reinvent and refine the product line and maintain its competitiveness against rival products.

The six principles are listed below, all of which capture both the spirit of the VAIO and of Sony's whole approach to innovation:

Doki-doki — Exhilaration
Mune-kyun — Passion
Waku waku — Stimulation
Koredayone — Differentiation
Daisuki — Cultivation
Hajimete — Innovation

OIL THE INNOVATION MACHINE

No doubt there is a fine art to the way Sony has marketed its brand into a global household name. But behind all the dazzling glitz and marketing slogans, what catches the consumers' hearts is the originality of Sony's products. At the core of the company's values is an absolute belief in originality and invention, not imitation. Perhaps sometimes that stubborn clinging to the idea of innovation works to the detriment of the corporation, as we have seen with the Chromatron project, for example. But this drive to create has also brought consumers Walkmans, Discmans, PlayStations and VAIO computers.

Some critics have argued that, in recent years, Sony has become sluggish and lost its reputation for being the first to come out with much of the technology available today. It wasn't the first to think about color televisions or laptop computers or handheld wireless organizers. But innovation isn't just about being the first to accomplish something. It is also about reinventing the ordinary and refining the existing. To quote Akio Morita, "If you go through life convinced that your way is always best, all the new ideas in the world will pass you by."[5] Sony's innovation machine is constantly spinning out something new, stretching the imagination of consumers, demanding that they think beyond what they know. A game console doesn't have to simply play games. It could also be a DVD player. A personal computer doesn't necessarily have to only be associated with dreary office work. It can be fun too. A mobile phone doesn't have to serve merely as a phone. It can be used to take digital photos that can be shared with friends instantly.

In the world of Sony, nothing has to be ordinary. Everything can be different. And engineers at Sony are challenged to reinvent and refine — whether it be making big smaller, making thick thinner or making a standard product more exciting. That is the secret to Sony's innovative success.

SONY'S RECIPES FOR SUCCESS

- *Innovate from the heart*: Some say inventors have an innate gift that cannot be learned. While that maybe true, one of the fundamental principles of innovation is one that can be acquired; that is, to put your heart into your work, putting the consumer's convenience and desires as priority when you innovate.

- *Trial and error*: No invention is perfect from the outset. Every product is a result of testing and refining. So you have to prepare for failures and be prepared to learn from them. Without taking risks, you will not discover better ways to make a product, in the processes, the materials, the wiring, and so on.

- *Create, don't copy*: To be original is far more challenging than to take what's already proven successful and make it well. But the rewards — both financial and in reputation — of creating your own products are also far greater. To have a solid base of your own technological know-how can also help you create more products and set the market trends in the future, giving you more power to influence and direct consumer behavior.

- *Reinvent and refine*: The best products are derived from years of tweaking and refining. Even a product like the personal computer, which has now been around for more than three decades, has undergone generations of change. In competitive industries such as the electronics and automobile sectors, constant improvements are necessary to keep ahead of your rivals. Sometimes these refinements are nothing more than a face-lift, an added function here or there. But an additional CD player in a car or a recording function on a DVD player makes all the difference in the consumers' eyes.

- *Think outside the box*: Do what others have never done before. Create products and services that may seem foreign to consumers. Don't just give consumers what they want today: create appetites for new gadgets, new services, things they may never have imagined could be possible.

NOTES

1.   *Genryu*, Sony Corporation of America, 1996.

2.   Nathan, op. cit.

3.   Sony Museum, Tokyo.

4.   Sheridan M. Tatsuno, *Created in Japan: from imitators to world-class innovators*, Harper & Row, 1990.

5.   Morita et al, op. cit.

Additional information in this chapter is drawn from interviews with Masanobu Sakaguchi, Jyungi Tsuyuki and Eiichi Yamamoto, Sony employees in the U.S. and Japan.

Four

PICKING A FIGHT: THE RISE OF SONY'S VIDEO-GAME BUSINESS

◆

In the early 1990s, thanks to the tenacity of engineer Ken Kutaragi, Sony made a decision to enter the cut-throat world of video games at a time when the field was utterly dominated by two companies, Sega and Nintendo. In four short years, Sony overcame the challenge of these two aggressive competitors to dominate the gaming industry. This chapter examines how Sony grew its video-game empire and illustrates the Sony tradition of balancing caution with fearless innovation.

Within two months of Sony's first foray into the home video-game industry in 1994, more than 300,000 units of the PlayStation game machines were sold in the United States, almost double the installed base of the Sega Corporation's Saturn console. With this initial success, Sony very quickly installed itself as a leader in a market that just a year before had been entirely foreign to the company. That Sony was able to secure its position so quickly in an industry dominated by successful multinationals is testimony to its ability to execute a risky and creative business strategy in a level-headed manner. It also shows the innovative fighting spirit embodied in Sony's corporate culture.

Much of PlayStation's success is due to Ken Kutaragi, now the chairman of Sony Computer Entertainment Inc. and the architect of Sony's gaming business. Kutaragi entirely fits Sony's pattern of venerated mavericks, irreverent and daring, and willing to bet on long shots that might turn into hits. His maverick streak follows a long tradition at Sony, one established by Ibuka (with his quest to develop Sony's own color-television technology) and Morita (with the Walkman project) themselves. Like the founders, Kutaragi persevered in the face of internal resistance and took what was already a common product, the video-game console, and created a revolutionary machine that would use compact-disc technology rather than cartridge, giving players crisper graphics and sound. The PlayStation has not only changed the landscape of the video-gaming industry, it has also brought Sony some of its biggest profits in the last two years.

KEN KUTARAGI

© Sony Computer Entertainment Inc.

Born   : August 8, 1950, Tokyo

Educated   : University   of   Electro-Communications, engineering, 1975

Career   : Joins Sony Corp. in 1975. Drafts plans for PlayStation in 1989, continuing after joint-venture partner Nintendo pulls out in 1991. Attracts hundreds of game developers and introduces first console in 1994.

Latest Move : PlayStation 2, which appears in Japan on March 4, 2000, powered by a 128-bit processor and synthesizer chip that deliver movie-quality graphics.

What's next : PlayStation 3, designed to integrate games, music and movies over broadband networks. Due by 2005

Source: Sony Computer Entertainment

Some say Sony was lucky that the video-gaming idea didn't occur to someone else working at the company. Most employees, however, would probably have abandoned the notion after their bosses dismissed it as a worthless toy. Not Kutaragi. An avid video-game player, he was ready to pick a fight with both the powerhouses of the industry, and with those who resisted within Sony. Sony's top management, who knew absolutely nothing about the video-game business, were skeptical of the prospects of success in video-gaming, and perhaps never thought that the division would create such a steady new line of revenues. Today, more than 500 million PlayStations have been sold worldwide. Sony Computer Entertainment, maker of the game console, accounts for more than 40 per cent of Sony's operating profits.[1]

The video-game business is notoriously cyclical, and has long been dominated by Japanese manufacturers. For more than two decades, the leader of the gaming industry had been Nintendo Corporation, which in 1983 launched Famicom, the game machine that quickly sold millions of units and spawned a generation of game-savvy kids. But the gaming industry is in no way sentimental, having learned that consumers can be fickle. It is a constant battle for dominance. As game machines age, sales of new game software created specifically for those machines taper off, and prices come down. Then new consoles and higher-priced new games come onto the market.

Each new generation of game consoles has a lifespan of about five years, analysts estimate, with operating profits peaking in the second half of the cycle, after hardware investments are amortized and before demand trails off. With the original PlayStation, Sony's operating profit margins for the game unit as a whole hit 17.4 per cent in 1998, four years after the system was introduced. But in today's competitive climate, the best Sony can hope for are 10 per cent profit margins on the PlayStation 2 by 2003, says one financial analyst in Tokyo who has followed Sony's businesses for more than a decade.

Still, the way Sony manages the PlayStation business is clearly a reflection of its innovative spirit to "reinvent, refine, and think outside the box". With each new generation of PlayStation game consoles, new features are introduced. When the first PlayStation was introduced, it was simply a game console, its sole purpose being the playing of video games. Today, the PlayStation 2 doubles up as a DVD player, with a network adapter that also allows players to get connected to the Internet.[2]

The Sony PlayStation story provides the most vivid demonstration that Sony nurtures ambitious engineers such as Kutaragi who challenge people's imagination, take risks and reach beyond the accepted realms of possibility. It also illustrates the challenges in store for the company as technology becomes increasingly standardized, reducing the breathing space between Sony and its competitors.

THE PLAYSTATION STORY

It all started with a broken contract in the late 1980s.

Kutaragi, then a Sony computer engineer with a passion for video games, proposed a console that would combine the graphic capabilities of a workstation with Sony's CD-ROM drive. For two years, Kutaragi searched without success for a champion anywhere within Sony's audiovisual group who would back his project. He moved himself and his research from one lab to another, hoping to find an advocate, until Teruo Tokunaka took him to see then-chairman Norio Ohga to pitch his idea.

Kutaragi had worked with Nintendo to develop an audio system for its console machine. Nintendo seemed to be a natural partner for Kutaragi's ambitious plan for a new kind of game console. When Nintendo jumped on board, Ohga gave Kutaragi the go-ahead to set up a joint-development team, and authorized him to develop a prototype. Ohga installed him in a corner of Sony Music Entertainment (Japan), and allowed him to fund his work with revenue Sony received from a sound processor that he developed earlier for Nintendo's Super 16 Bit Cartridge. But, in 1992, Nintendo pulled out abruptly, leaving Kutaragi in the lurch.[3]

FOLLOW YOUR HEART

Being a latecomer in a developed and competitive market is tough. But if you have the conviction and the belief that you can succeed, and a solid business plan, you may even outsmart more-established players. Sometimes, persistence is the crucial and missing piece of a business execution. Follow your heart. Often, with a solid strategy, you have little to lose. Kutaragi had no background in the video-game business. He was just an avid fan of video games. But he had a dream of what he could do with Sony's audio and visual technologies. He believed he could make a machine that would outsmart the existing ones. His persistence and belief in his dream gave Sony and consumers today's PlayStation.

When Ohga confronted Nintendo President Hiroshi Yamauchi, the latter denied any knowledge of a binding agreement. Ohga was furious and regarded Nintendo's change of heart as an affront to his company. Kutaragi still wanted to pursue the project, which meant huge risks for Sony, which had no prior experience in the video-gaming industry. Many top executives spoke out against the plan, arguing that it was too risky, and a video-game console business did not provide any synergies with the rest of Sony's electronics product line. Sony simply didn't have the experience or the knowledge to succeed in the gaming industry. But Ohga, incensed by Nintendo's sudden pull-out, went against much internal opposition and his own reservations to approve Kutaragi's plans to develop a game console that would give Nintendo, the maker of the world's most popular game machine, a run for its money.

But there was more to it than revenge. Kutaragi swore to leave if Sony refused to pursue his dream. Ohga felt that Kutaragi, considered to be one of Sony's brightest engineers, was too valuable to let go and gave him the green light. That decision has paid off.

Today, in the United States, one in four households has a PlayStation. According to International Data Corporation, Sony currently controls more than 50 per cent of the console market. Two-thirds of all video games sold over the past four years were for the PlayStation.

A DIFFERENT SONY BEAST

Within Sony, the PlayStation division was a different beast. In creating the gaming unit, Ohga allowed Kutaragi almost total control over the strategy and the direction of the game-console business. Sony PlayStation had its own separate design and development teams and its own factories that make the chips for the console. (Sony's semiconductor unit was not included in the project initially.) Such autonomy was unusual within Japanese companies, and Sony was praised for allowing the hard-charging, sometimes-volatile Kutaragi free rein. Rather than stifling Kutaragi's idiosyncrasies, Sony cultivated them, allowing him to set up the PlayStation operations in Akasaka, a bustling neighborhood known for its restaurants and night life, rather than in industrial Shinagawa.

Kutaragi was also allowed to establish a compensation system at Sony Computer Entertainment that was tied far more to performance than elsewhere in the company. Sony's public relations people learned to bite their

> Kutaragi was a "Michael Jackson" of the game world.
> — Sony executive

tongues as he repeatedly criticized the corporation for its stodginess — even while noting that the only place in Japan he could have realized his full potential was at Sony. But Ohga did try to counterbalance the fiery Kutaragi by dispatching two trusted lieutenants to look after him. Over the years, they refereed a lot of disputes. When, for example, the head of Sony's U.S. games business grew fed up with Kutaragi's micromanagement, one of the executives penned the manager a sharp letter telling him to obey Kutaragi. The unit's founder, the executive wrote, was a "Michael Jackson" of the game world — quirky but creative.[4]

For Ohga to allow Kutaragi such independence was unprecedented even within Sony, a more progressive and risk-taking company than most Japanese companies. On the one hand, he allowed Kutaragi to proceed with the project because he didn't want to lose a bright engineer. But some industry observers familiar with the discussions within Sony at the time also believe that the independence the PlayStation division received distanced it from the company's core electronics business and thus, in a way, helped protect the Sony group as a whole from being overly exposed to the risk of a possible failure. At the time, many Sony executives bet that the game-console division wouldn't take off, seeing little hope of it being able to compete with Sega and Nintendo, the established giants of the industry. Such was Sony's hesitation that the original PlayStation didn't bear Sony's logo and branding. Not until the second generation of PlayStation 1, after the CD-enabled Sony game console took the industry by surprise and gained huge popularity, did Sony start heavily marketing the game console as its own.

UNDERSTAND YOUR ENEMY'S WEAKNESSES

When Sony decided to go solo in developing a game console in 1993, its biggest disadvantage was that it was the latest comer, and one with no previous experience in video

Original PlayStation, 1994 — © Sony Computer Entertainment Inc.

gaming. Sega and Nintendo had both carved out their market share and target audience, establishing long-term relationships with software developers and retail distributors. The question Sony faced was: Where do we fit in? To succeed would mean stealing market share from the gaming giants — and that would be a daunting task.

Sony's strategy was quite simple and logical: to search out the enemy's weaknesses and turn them into advantages for themselves, a common tactic for a latecomer to any commercial market (and one that it would use again later when it introduced its VAIO computer and Clié handheld organizer). Shigeo Maruyama, one of Kutaragi's trusted colleagues and now vice-president of Sony Computer Entertainment, explained at the time: "We needed to find out what Nintendo was planning to do, find out what software companies, retailers and users find fault in with Nintendo, and then we needed to propose a solution and a strategy that would solve their problems."

Getting Namco Inc., one of the key game-software developers, to sign onto Sony's PlayStation team was an amazing feat and marked the beginning of a strong run of popular video games made for PlayStation. Namco was drawn to Sony by the possibility of creating ground-breaking three-dimensional graphics. But the major reason Namco signed up was because its relationship with Nintendo, Sony's biggest competitor, had become strained — a fact that Sony capitalized on to its benefit.

When Nintendo first introduced Famicom, Namco's Pacman and Zebius games, both written for Famicom, they quickly became the most popular games, earning the software developer the award as Nintendo's most prized developer. For five years, Namco enjoyed elite treatment by Nintendo, and through preferential treatment made a large profit. But when Super Famicom was introduced in 1990, Nintendo demoted Namco to ordinary developer status, forcing it to compete with other software developers and immediately affecting Namco's bottom line.[5]

"We needed to find out what Nintendo was planning to do, find out what software companies, retailers and users find fault in with Nintendo, and then we needed to propose a solution and a strategy that would solve their problems."
— Shigeo Maruyama, vice-president, Sony Computer Entertainment

PlayStation's appearance on the video-gaming scene was timely for Namco, which had already started experimenting with three-dimensional graphics. So when Kutaragi approached Namco with a proposition to develop unprecedented three-dimensional graphics video games, it was a natural deal, a matter of the right timing and the right pitch. To Sony's delight, Namco even stopped writing software for Nintendo in order to focus on PlayStation games. It has now written numerous games for PlayStation, including Ridge Racer and Tekken, two of the initial games that have been refined and re-issued for the various generations of Sony PlayStations.

UNDERSTAND YOUR STRENGTHS

In the video-gaming business, the most vital component for success is the game software. No matter how sophisticated the game console is, without the breadth and quality of games available, it would be hard to draw a critical mass of players. Software licensing fees are also where the profits lie. The actual hardware — the console itself — tends to be a loss-making product for the first few years of its life. Software makes up for the losses.

Sony realized this early on, and its primary goal with respect to PlayStation software was to maximize the number and variety of titles. Whereas Nintendo and, to some extent, Sega had always restricted the number of software titles and enforced strict quality and content standards, Sony was willing to license any PlayStation software that didn't cause the hardware to "crash". This approach was partially a result of Sony's experience with its Betamax video-cassette technology, and in a way a demonstration of learning from its own mistakes. Although the Betamax standard for video cassettes was, in most assessments, a superior technology to the VHS standard, it lost out to VHS in good part due to a lack of compatible videos for Sony Betamax machines. Because of this experience, Sony was determined to support PlayStation with as many software titles as possible. (Sony bought Columbia TriStar Pictures in 1989 for the same reason — owning a library of movie titles that could hopefully provide the synergy with its electronics devices.)

Almost from the beginning, PlayStation's software titles outnumbered Sega's Saturn titles by four-to-one, despite Saturn's four-month head start. PlayStation software also targeted a more mature audience than the traditional core video-game market of 10–16-year-old boys. Early PlayStation hits included advanced sports games, such as NFL GameDay, and fighting games, such as Mortal Kombat 3, which included graphic violence that failed to meet the content standards of Nintendo. According to Andrew House, executive vice-president of Sony Computer Entertainment America, "We've dignified video games. It's OK to be 30 and to play video games."

To support PlayStation with the breadth of software titles, Sony realized early on that, unlike Sega, it did not have the resources to write its own game software. It would need to rely on third-party software developers for content. Kutaragi and his team believed at the time that the strength of Sony was that it would be the first to introduce CD-based game consoles. Using CD technology, the games would be able to feature crisper and enhanced graphics and ground-breaking three-dimensional art. At the time, three-dimensional graphics were the ultimate dream for software developers. Namco had already started experimenting with its arcade games, but three-dimensional graphics for home-computer games still seemed out of reach for most developers. Sony's ambition was to combine three-dimensional graphics with CD technology, entirely new territory in the video-gaming industry as both Sega and Nintendo consoles used cartridges for their games.

"We've dignified video games. It's OK to be 30 and to play video games." — Andrew House, executive vice-president, Sony Computer Entertainment, America

Between May and August 1993, Kutaragi led a team of developers to visit more than a hundred game-software companies. During the course of their visits, they tried to meet both managerial staff and developers, believing that PlayStation's technological advances would attract the developers, who would in turn try to persuade their managers to join Sony's project. But in these initial meetings, the PlayStation team never got to meet developers and the managers basically told them that they were going in way over their heads. One software company manager told the Sony team that three-dimensional graphics could not possibly be realized for at least another decade and, if Sony were to enter this line of business without the necessary background and knowledge, it was bound to fail. Another software executive basically laid out the criteria for cooperation: that PlayStation had to prove it could be a viable competitor in the market, meaning that it would have to sell more than three million consoles. That goal was a realistic one considering that Nintendo's Super Famicom had sold about eight million consoles at the time. The challenge posed a bit of "a chicken or egg" dilemma. Sony needed software developers to get on board in order for Sony to attract consumers to buy the console. Without games, the console was essentially useless.

Not much progress was made in securing partnerships with game developers, but these meetings with the software companies were not entirely wasted. In talking with them, Kutaragi and his team gathered better intelligence on which companies would eventually be interested in three-dimensional graphics. The challenge then became how to arouse their interest enough to get them on board with the PlayStation project.

Surprisingly, it was Sega, one of Sony's chief rivals, that gave PlayStation its much-needed boost. In late August 1993, Sega introduced an arcade game using three-dimensional graphics that stunned the game-software developers, and made them realize that the possibility of three-dimensional graphics was not as distant as they had thought. When Sony introduced its own three-dimensional-graphics-enabled arcade machines at a trade show later that year, the attitude toward Sony changed drastically. Knowing now that it was possible to develop three-dimensional graphics in video games, people began to ask questions, curious about how they could get involved.

The clincher came in 1996 when Square Company decided to put its "Final Fantasy" game on Sony's fledging PlayStation, abandoning long-time partner Nintendo. The deal helped vault Sony past Nintendo as the world's leading game-console maker and it retains its spot, with some 70 per cent of the market for consoles hooked up to TVs.

Everybody's Golf 3 — © Sony Computer Entertainment Inc.

MARKETING GENIUS

From the day it was launched, the PlayStation has projected an aura of hipness. For one thing, Sony largely ignored Nintendo's sub-teen and teen following and zoned in on older customers, offering racier, more complex games. Sony understood something very distinctly Sony: creating a market demand where there didn't seem to be one before. The technological innovation is undoubtedly the most crucial element in this success formula. But, according to many analysts, Kutaragi's technological creativity was complemented by the marketing genius of Akira Sato, now chief operating officer at Sony Computer Entertainment.

GUERILLA MARKETING: CREATING THE BUZZ

Glossy posters and punchy commercials that cost millions often can do the trick for companies wanting to promote a new product. But sometimes a more effective method is simple, old-fashioned, word of mouth. By homing in on the target audience and winning their favor, you can start a successful marketing campaign simply by relying on them to tell their friends. Word passes from one to another and soon there is a buzz about the product.

How Sony harnessed guerilla marketing tactics to PlayStation's cause is amply illustrated by its launch in the United Kingdom in 1995. Before the launch, one in four males between the ages of eight and 50 owned a Sega; Sega's Sonic the Hedgehog and Nintendo's Super Mario were ubiquitous characters, with Atari, Philips and Commodore attempting, unsuccessfully, to muscle in on the action.

Then, out of nowhere, Sony trounced them all. It was a masterly marketing drive.[6]

Having learned from the failure of the Betamax video format that there was no point in producing superior hardware if there wasn't the software to back it up, Sony was determined that the entire package of console and games would be in place at launch. Managers in the U.K. and Japan wined and dined software developers to convince them to come on board. All of Sony's efforts paid off, so that by the time it was due to launch, the company had not only bought game developer Psygnosis, but also brought influential software developers, such as Electronic Arts, and independent retailers on to its side.

The challenge was to generate interest among players, most of whom had already established loyalties to the Sega and Nintendo consoles. The PlayStation was aimed at 18–24-year-olds who appreciated the vivid graphics, the sophisticated games and the CD-quality music offered by the console, and who had outgrown Game Boy. The thinking was this: here was a sexy purchase they could get excited about. And, once hooked, Sony reasoned, they'd bring their brothers and dads on board, too. The strategy was simple: word of mouth. Hand out as many PlayStations as possible to opinion formers and let them do the rest of the work. In all, about 5,000 were given away in the U.K. Sony also put a PlayStation chill-out room in the Ministry of Sound, a hip London club. It cost Sony £10,000, but it led to 43 other U.K. clubs installing their own PlayStation rooms. Student unions followed suit.

Then, Sony put together videos featuring clips from the best PlayStation games with avant-garde music and distributed them to 450 U.K. clubs as well as festivals like Big Love, reaching out to possibly a million potential PlayStation players. The message that Sony wanted to get across was the power of PlayStation. Here would be a game console that would do everything that other game machines did: you could play all kinds of games — hunting, fighting, racing, you name it — but on the PlayStation, the sound quality, the graphics quality and the sophistication of the game were all better.

DIRECT DISTRIBUTION

One of the problems Nintendo had in competing with PlayStation was the fact that Nintendo was sold and marketed through a network of distributors. By selling through a middleman, it was difficult for Nintendo to direct and control its brand image and its customer-service quality. In Japan, for example, distributors in the Nintendo network bought the games from Nintendo and then sold the game software and consoles to retailers. With this system, the distributors are under tremendous pressure to control inventory. For unpopular games, there is the urgent need to get rid of stock quickly, at any cost. For popular games, there is an incentive to release the games slowly to force prices to go up with the high demand. The uneven treatment of Nintendo games turned out to hurt the brand's image. The same problem prevailed in Europe. Nintendos were sold and marketed in Europe via a distributor, The Games. One editor of a Nintendo 64 game title complained that The Games was trying to muscle in on the older PlayStation market, while ignoring the fact that its software titles and Nintendo's wholesome image failed to appeal to this age group. Sony, on the other hand, had control of all operational processes — from manufacture to marketing — making it simpler for retailers to handle Sony's product. It has also meant Sony has been able to maintain a higher profile in the trade than its competitors and its trade pitch has been complemented by its marketing strategy. One spin-off of establishing a direct rapport with independent retailers was that Sony developed a network of informers and was warned of software launches and price cuts from other competitors and could, in turn, undercut them. It also meant competitors like Nintendo and Sega were always trying to catch up.

REINVENT YOURSELF, REINVENT THE INDUSTRY

Even as the PlayStation vaulted past Nintendo's machine as the best-selling game console in 1994, Kutaragi was already planning bigger things. A chart he prepared in the early 1990s named a big future competitor: Microsoft Corp. The prediction came at least five years before Microsoft conceived its game-machine plans.

Two years after the first PlayStation consoles hit the shelves, Kutaragi assembled top engineers from Sony and its partner, semiconductor maker Toshiba Corp., at a beach resort near Tokyo. He told those present he wanted a next-generation machine with performance that surpassed that of the personal computer and that had 10-times the graphics-processing power of the first PlayStation. He code-named the project "Godzilla" to emphasize his thirst for computing power.

Kutaragi eventually got what he wanted — a game console so powerful it can perform physics calculations on the same level as advanced scientific computers. This processing power is applied to churning out video images, which for players means lifelike and heart-racing games. The PlayStation 2 features a DVD player, bringing the Sony game console much closer to a vision of the PlayStation as a platform for interactive entertainment, including the ability to download music, movies and surf the Internet.

But the complexity of PlayStation 2 meant added difficulty and cost for software writers who created the games. Some game developers have said that it will take several years for them to adjust to the power of the new machine, which is driven by a Toshiba processor built to Sony's specifications. What's more, the PlayStation 2 has certain quirks that make creating games even harder. As a result, most PlayStation 2 titles have largely been retreads of older games.

When PlayStation 2 was first released in 2000, it flew off the retail shelves, but a glitch in the production line made it hard to meet the tremendous demand. Kutaragi had forced engineers to design a Sony-built chip, called the Graphics Synthesizer, that had proven to be something of a bugbear. Low yields at Sony factories producing the chip forced Sony to halve the number of PlayStation 2 it could deliver for the crucial Christmas launch. But Sony executives say that these were normal start-up problems. They say the company has ironed out production problems and has been ramping up the number of game titles available, such as Grand Theft Auto III, Gran Turismo 3 and Madden NFL 2003. Despite these hiccups, the brilliance of PlayStation 2 was never lost. It introduced a brand new kind of thinking to the world of game consoles — expanding the possibilities beyond game-playing to incorporate watching DVDs and surfing the Internet.[7]

PlayStation 2, 2000 — © Sony Computer Entertainment Inc.

Already Sony is preparing the next generation of PlayStations — PlayStation 3. It has said it is working with IBM Corp. and Toshiba Corp. to design a processor for the new machine that will be as much as 1,000-times more powerful than the PlayStation 2 and built for broadband networking. The chip will function as both a network server and a game processor, and reside either at a central location or in hardware in individual homes. This will change the whole impression of what a game console should be. Instead of just serving as a machine to play interactive video games with friends, it will also be able to replace the DVD player, and possibly, should Kutaragi's vision be realized, the home desktop computer. And games, Kutaragi envisions, will eventually no longer come in packages, arriving or being played directly with other gamers over speedy fiber-optic links.

BREAKING NEW GROUND: GAMING CHALLENGES IN THE FUTURE

With the advent of the Internet and the slow but sure growth of broadband usage around the world, Kutaragi and his team are eyeing the Internet as a new market to develop. Sony has touted the intention to turn the game machine into platforms for interactive gaming and other services such as music download. The continuing scarcity of homes with high-speed connections to the Internet is a major obstacle. Currently, broadband penetration in the U.S., PlayStation's single largest market, is still less than 15 per cent. In Japan, one of the most technologically advanced societies, broadband usage is only beginning to pick up. In fact, online gaming has really taken off only in South Korea, a country with the highest broadband penetration in the world.

Nevertheless, Sony Computer Entertainment's plans for online gaming in the U.S. have certainly intensified the market battle with Microsoft and Nintendo Co. in the video-game business. The network adapter Sony introduced for the 2002 holiday season in the U.S. — partly prompted by Microsoft's XBox broadband capabilities — works with any Internet service provider, and Sony's installation CD includes software for automatically setting up customers of popular American online services such as America Online and Earthlink. The adapter also came with one free game, Twisted Metal Black Online, to whet consumers' appetites for online games. This will at first involve playing opponents over the Internet and eventually include downloading everything from additional game content to music and video. For now, online console-games will work in much the same way as most PC games run: consumers buy a disc with both an offline version of the game and a version that can be played for free online. One of the biggest challenges online PlayStation games will face, analysts say, is the question of where to store the games. Sony has not yet set a date for making an add-on hard drive for the PlayStation 2 to allow consumers to store their downloaded games from the Internet. In Japan, Kutaragi has also linked up with four ISPs to jointly run a high-speed online-game service built around the PlayStation 2, and is exploring possibilities with Japanese telecom giant NTT DoCoMo Co. to find game connectivity with third-generation (3G) mobile phones.[8]

Whether the PlayStation division can secure a profit-making business model and market interest in downloadable online games will be a test of how PlayStation will survive in an increasingly networked world. The overall impression, analysts say, is that Sony is still working out its online strategy, even as it faces competitive pressure from Microsoft, which has said it will introduce an online service for its XBox game console. "Gamers traditionally go out and buy memory cards and maybe an extra controller, and that's about it," says one gaming analyst. "I think Sony clearly needs to demonstrate the value proposition to get people to buy the network adapter."

SONY ONLINE ENTERTAINMENT

Although Sony Computer Entertainment is only just beginning to introduce an online gaming community, elsewhere in Sony that has already become a reality. In the summer of 1995, Sony Pictures Digital Entertainment launched a new online division, Sony Online Entertainment, an interactive entertainment network, which creates, develops and provides online games for the personal computer, online and console markets.

Working independently from Sony Computer Entertainment, the San Diego-based Sony Online Entertainment has developed the only successfully distributed online games, ranging from simple card and trivia games to more strategic, tactical and role-playing interactive worlds. Its online game, Everquest, has sold more than a million copies worldwide. Everquest's online community has more than 425,000 paying subscribers, who each pay US$12.95 a month. Launched in March 1999, Everquest brings players into the world of Norrath, where players embark on perilous and exciting journeys through a fantasy world. The game allows players to create their own specialized characters by selecting from 12 races and 14 classes, skills, physical appearances, names and religions. According to International Data Corporation, Everquest has become the world's leading multi-player online game, with players in the U.S., England, Canada, Japan, Taiwan, Korea, Saudi Arabia, Germany, France, Italy and Australia. Sony Online Entertainment says Everquest holds 52 per cent of the market share in online gaming, with 90,000 players online at any one moment. The average subscriber spends about 20 hours a week on EverQuest.

Sony Online Entertainment's website, www.station.com, has more than 13 million registered users. In May 2000, the company acquired and fully integrated Verant Interactive to further strengthen Sony's position in multi-player online gaming. This now allows game enthusiasts to play games online, find online teammates and opponents, attend organized fan events (both in game and in real life), join communities, forums, chat rooms and message boards, and more.

Sony Computer Entertainment's own development of online games will certainly affect the survival of Sony Online Entertainment. Sony Online Entertainment officials say that they design games that are also geared toward PlayStation's platform. But, analysts say, once PlayStation's online gaming model reaches a critical mass, the question may be asked about the fate of either online service or whether they should be merged. A merger would also be a test of how well two Sony subsidiaries can collaborate, in particular Sony Computer Entertainment, which has largely worked independently of other Sony companies.

THE GRAND VISION OF BROADBAND ENTERTAINMENT

From the beginning, Sony Computer Entertainment has been largely independent from the rest of the Sony group. The division started off as a joint venture with Sony Music before it morphed into an independent Sony-owned subsidiary. (When current chairman Nobuyuki Idei became Sony president in 1995, he decided to dissolve the joint venture and make the games business a unit of Sony's main company. Kutaragi rebelled but was overruled.) According to industry analysts, the independence of Sony Computer

Entertainment — from its design team and engineers, to the manufacturing of PlayStation semiconductor chips and the marketing — has been a key reason for PlayStation's success. Kutaragi and his team have been able to create the exact game console they wanted to the specifications they envisioned. This independence made sense at the time; Sony Computer Entertainment was involved in a business quite different from the audio-visual, electronics side of the operations.

However, given Idei's vision of a new Sony, one with great hardware that spawns even more exciting and much more profitable software, the parent company has to bring Sony Computer Entertainment closer into the fold. Not surprisingly, Kutaragi didn't try to hide his disapproval of his unit's loss of independence. In 1999, he stunned his bosses and colleagues when he told a meeting of Sony executives that "the old guys should step aside to make way for the young". And he would comment again in an interview with *Forbes* magazine in 2001: "I wish SCE was an independent company again." This brought an unusually severe response from Idei, who told *Forbes* that same year: "If Kutaragi says anything more, he will be fired. As long as he is successful, he has freedom, but if he slips up, then he is out."

Since then, Sony Computer Entertainment officials say there has been closer collaboration with the electronics side of the business, including involving the electronics side in the development of the semiconductor processor that will be part of PlayStation 3. However, the marketing of the game console will probably still remain separate from other products, they say, particularly because PlayStation is primarily a game product and it would be difficult to combine its marketing strategies with those of the rest of Sony's product line. But with Idei's vision of a broadband, networked world, and with PlayStation playing a key role as a server platform, the collaboration should become tighter. Already, there is a dilemma within Sony of how to juggle the synergies between Sony Computer Entertainment's plans for online gaming and the online-gaming division of Sony Digital Pictures Entertainment, a subsidiary of Sony Pictures Entertainment, which is already a proven hit among gamers in the U.S.

SONY'S RECIPES FOR SUCCESS

- *Never give up*: If you believe you have a good idea, don't give up because you've met some internal resistance to it. Do your homework, research the market, and come up with good arguments for how your idea would benefit the company.

- *Allow room for risks and exploration*: Embarking on a new business idea can be nerve-racking. You have to allow room for your business development team to explore ideas and strategies to launch new products or services. Control too tightly, and you risk suffocating the new idea, and contributing to its failure. Control too little, and you risk watching the idea spin out of control. (It is a delicate balance that needs to be managed carefully.)

- *Understand your enemy's weaknesses*: When you enter a new market already saturated by strong players, you have to really do your homework. Where are your enemy's weaknesses? Are there dissatisfied consumers or suppliers or retailers? Why? How can you make life easier for them? Seize those weaknesses and turn them into your strengths.

- *Understand your strengths*: You may be entering a new market substantially different from your core businesses, but that doesn't mean you don't have strengths and past successes you can draw upon to help you strategize. Leverage what you're good at and apply your strengths to your new business strategies.

- *Brand it! Promote it!*: Often, a product's success comes from word of mouth or what some in the marketing industry call "buzz". Create a buzz for your product. Decide who will be your most obvious fans. Gain their favor and promote it through them.

- *Reinvent and refine*: Initial success doesn't guarantee lasting success. Keep reinventing and refining your products. Make them better, more memorable, more consumer-friendly. There is always room for improvement.

NOTES

1. "Sony Changes the Game", Fast Company, August 1997.

2. "Competitive Dynamics in Home Video Games (I): The Sony PlayStation", Harvard Business School.

3. Reiji Asakura, *Revolutionaries at Sony: The Making of the Sony PlayStation and the Visionaries Who Conquered the World of Video Games*, McGraw-Hill, 2000.

4. Robert A. Guth, "Sony Grooms Games Maverick for Next Level of Management", *The Wall Street Journal*, November 18, 2002.

5. Dyan Machan, "Great Job — You're fired", *Forbes*, September 23, 1996.

6. Sue Beenstock, "Marketing Focus: Market raider: How Sony won the console game: Sony's rise to the top has left rivals fighting for a slice of the action", *Marketing*, September 10, 1998.

7. Robert A. Guth and Khanh T.L. Tran, "Game Battle Claims a Casualty — Sega to Exit Player Market, Sony's Problems Continue As Industry Sales Flatten", *The Wall Street Journal*, January 31, 2001.

8. David Becker, "Holes found in Sony's online game plan", CNET News.

Additional information in this chapter is taken from interviews with Kenichi Fukunaga, Yoshiko Furusawa and Nanako Kato, Sony employees in the U.S. and Japan.

Five

CONNECTING THE DOTS: MAKING SYNERGY WORK

The pursuit of synergy pervades the management of most large companies. But how corporations can maximize cross-business synergies is also one of the greatest challenges for businesses today. Corporations can no longer offer stand-alone products or services and expect to be profitable because now is the era of the one-stop shop. Sony is no exception. With current chairman Nobuyuki Idei's vision of Sony becoming a broadband entertainment giant, this challenge is ever more crucial to resolve. This chapter talks about the making of today's multi-business Sony Corporation.

"Synergy" — this "S" word is considered taboo within Sony. Chairman Nobuyuki Idei prefers to label the idea of creating internal collaborations between Sony businesses as "creating a value chain". But call it what you may, Sony, like many modern-day corporations, has little choice but to pursue this path. Sony got rich and famous by building a series of great gadgets (the transistor radio, the Walkman, the Trinitron, to name a few) to distinguish itself initially from competitors. Although Sony still makes money on its electronic gadgets, its competitive edge in such stand-alone products is fading in a world where music and video are increasingly being rendered in the digital language of computers, and technology know-how is becoming standardized. As one financial analyst puts it, Sony's profit margins on traditional electronic gadgets are now "peanuts". Only the red-hot PlayStation video-game business is bringing in profits for the company, making up 42 per cent of its operating profits in 1999, for example, even though it only comprised 15 per cent of total sales. Even so, the gaming business is posing something of a question as Microsoft and its souped-up XBox present a formidable challenge. Any downturn in the gaming industry could easily shake the financial base of the entire Sony organization.

The way out, as Idei sees it, is to provide the missing link between Sony's "content" — its music, films and games — and the delivery side of the business — everything from TVs and audio gear to trendy movie theaters. This is a strategy that means amassing networking skills, and one that other media giants such as AOL Time Warner and Vivendi Universal have contemplated and attempted, thus far with limited success. With the rules of the business world changing, so must Sony. Masaru Ibuka was a transistor kid. His co-founder Akio Morita was the Walkman kid. Norio Ohga was the CD kid. But today, the founders' era, and for that matter, the analog era that Sony capitalized on is coming to an end. When Idei assumed leadership at Sony in 1995, he came up with his very own new label: Digital Dream Kid. Digital technology has propelled the electronics business to light speed. Sony now has to run against computer giants such as Compaq and IBM in the race to develop software, engage in complex battles over copyrights and industry standards in the entertainment business, and frame alliances and joint ventures before rivals intercede. The winners will be decided not simply by techno-vision but also by sniffing out the truffles in these daunting challenges and bringing them to market. Idei believes the solution will come with trying to bring together Sony's hardware and content businesses to develop a well-rounded package in which Sony content runs on Sony devices in the home, and new e-business schemes can collect transaction fees from consumers tapping Sony's rich pools of content — whether it's watching a movie on a giant digital television or buying a movie ticket on a website tapped from a sleek Sony VAIO notebook computer.

To accomplish this, consumers must be able to enter Sony's digital world, whether it's from a TV, a PC or a cell phone. The groundwork has already been laid out for Idei's "New Sony" — Sony has a movie studio, a record label and a thriving video-gaming business. Now Idei must bring the content side of the business closer to Sony's core electronics business. But synergies between business divisions are notoriously challenging to manage. Royal Dutch/Shell Group's initial attempt to launch a common credit card across Europe failed. Allegis, United Airlines Inc.'s bid to build synergies in related travel businesses like hotels and airlines, was quickly dismantled. The truth is, for most corporations, the arithmetic of cross-business synergies does not add up. Part of the problem is that corporations often don't think through why they need to have synergies and how the connections across business units will help the corporation in the long run. Sometimes business units that seem to have intuitive synergies end up locking horns with one another. A further challenge lies in the fact that when companies acquire businesses outside their expertise, they are competing with rivals that have been in the business for years and thus have much more experience and knowledge. Even though corporations usually acquire people who know the business, integrating new businesses into the parent group is never easy.

> The winners will be decided not simply by techno-vision but also by sniffing out the truffles in these daunting challenges and bringing them to market.

One of the most crucial points in this respect is figuring out where the new business stands in relation to the parent group. For Sony, figuring out all these dynamics between its businesses is perhaps the most pressing challenge — and it is not simply a matter of business units getting along with one another. At the core of this, the identity of the corporation is at stake.[1]

Is Sony a consumer-electronics company anymore? Or is it an entertainment company? Or both? Today's world is dominated by a new breed of consumers who are raised not by the television but by the Internet, with no loyalties to the analog technology of the past, to the Sony name or anything else. For these new consumers, the old rules that governed society no longer apply. Every rule written in the age of analog needs now to be re-examined, and some turned inside out, to accommodate the digital age. In many ways, Sony has to rebuild a new foundation on top of the old, one that will be tough enough to withstand the test of the digital future.

BEFORE SYNERGY, DIVERSIFICATION

The current emphasis many global corporations have placed on capturing synergies is a clear indication that they are diversifying. There are those who believe that corporations should focus on what they are good at — their "core competence" — and let other companies to do the rest of the job. But in Sony's case, the consumer-electronics industry's thinning profit margins and the increasing standardization of technology basically give the company little choice but to search for alternative sources of revenue. Sony is still fighting the noble battle in consumer electronics, focusing on the branding, marketing and details of the product that make it a distinctly Sony gadget, better and above the rest of the generics. But that alone is no longer enough to ensure its survival, as, perhaps, the Betamax incident served to illustrate.

Sony spent a large part of the mid 1970s fighting a legal battle in the U.S. Supreme Court to prove that home taping is legal and not an infringement of copyrights. But when it won a Supreme Court ruling in 1984, it was a rather hollow victory. Sony soon discovered that even the world's best hardware does not necessarily sell unless the content appeals to consumers. While Sony bet on Betamax, the rest of Japan's consumer-electronics industry were embracing the VHS. As more people bought VHS machines, more production houses turned out VHS cassettes and Sony watched its product starve to death for lack of software. (Sony still makes Beta-format VCRs, mainly for export to the Third World.) Morita believed at the time that Sony's Betamax might have prevailed if the company had been able to provide an attractive line of movies and content to complement the machine.

After Betamax, it was clear that the company needed to diversify and do so urgently. But diversifying is a high-stakes game with extraordinary rewards and risks. Success stories abound — think of General Electric Company, Disney Enterprises Inc. and 3M Corp. — but so do such infamous and costly failures as Quaker Oats Company's entry into (and rapid exit from) the fruit juice business with Snapple Beverage Corporation, and Radio Corporation of America's forays into computers, carpets and rental cars. Before diversifying, corporations have to consider not just what their company does, but about what it does better than its competitors. Like good chess players, forward-thinking corporations have to think two or three moves ahead. They have to ask themselves whether they are content merely to be a player in a new market or whether they want to emerge as a winner. In considering this question, the issue of profitability comes up. No company, of course, intentionally diversifies into an industry in which it will lose money. But corporations considering a new market venture must decide how much money they want to make and how well this venture will work with what the rest of the corporation does.

Sony's foray into video games, as discussed in the previous chapter, is a nice example of how it entered unfamiliar territory and ultimately won. With PlayStation, Sony recognized what it did best — thinking outside the box and taking risks — and introduced new possibilities in the video-game industry. PlayStation 2 pushed the envelope even more by making it possible to have a game console and DVD player, all in one package. Although at the outset Sony knew little about the video-gaming industry, the inexperience actually worked to its advantage. The end result was a well-made, nicely designed machine that was technologically more sophisticated than any of the more entrenched competitors. When a corporation can achieve this, even as a latecomer to a market, it has succeeded in diversifying. The same pattern of innovation and risk-taking was also evident in the company's forays into the computer and handheld-organizer markets.

But Sony's diversification was not always a smooth ride. PlayStation, the VAIO computer and the Clié handheld organizer all had one thing in common — they all fell within the realm of electronics gadgetry, where Sony's core strengths lie. But Betamax inspired more than just diversification within the electronics industry. Morita wanted software, and that meant reaching beyond the company's traditional areas of strength. His eventual purchases of CBS Records Inc., which already operated a joint venture with Sony in Japan, and of Columbia TriStar Pictures were made with this very idea of content diversification in mind.[2]

But diversifying into the entertainment industry is a very different matter from diversification within Sony's familiar electronics realm. This is where the idea of creating synergies — inter-unit ties — becomes crucial and challenging.

WHAT MAKES SYNERGY WORK?

Diversifying and capturing synergies go hand in hand. As you diversify, you have to think of how you would integrate the new businesses into the overall corporate framework. A corporation may branch into a new market with great success, but unless the new business can directly benefit and complement the corporation's business model, the benefits will only go so far. This is a tricky dilemma that Sony is trying to resolve.

Sony has its hand in electronics, movies, music, video games and even online banking and insurance. How they all fit together has yet to be fully realized. That this hasn't yet been completely resolved is a product of Sony's global localization philosophy, which has left all these major business units to operate independently of one another, often creating tensions between the different businesses. This is evident in the uncertain relationship between the Tokyo headquarters and Sony Computer Entertainment, which we examined in the previous chapter. It is also evident in Sony's movie business at Columbia TriStar Pictures, which will be studied in greater depth in the next chapter.

The word "synergy" is derived from the Greek word *synergos*, and means "working together". In business usage, synergy typically refers to the ability of two or more units or companies to generate greater value working together than they could if they worked separately. Most business synergies take one of six forms: sharing knowledge; coordinating strategies; sharing resources; coordinating the flow of products to reduce inventory costs; pooling negotiating power; or creating new businesses together. Like most rules of business, there is no one right way to capture synergies that work. Too many forced links between business units could actually restrict creativity and inhibit the agility of individual units, creating in the process a lumbering giant. On the other hand, too little collaboration can cause a company to miss important opportunities. The advent of the Internet complicates further the process by which a corporation might discover synergies between its businesses.

Half of the battle when it comes to creating synergy is to have a clear road map of what you want out of your different business units.

Sometimes, as we will see later in this chapter, corporations will find themselves competing internally with online and bricks-and-mortar business units vying for the same business or locking horns on business strategies. Such things challenge a corporation's ability to achieve synergies smoothly. By the same token, an appropriate amount of inter-unit competition could also be beneficial to corporations. For example, competition between online and bricks-and-mortar counterparts could catalyze growth for the company as a whole or uncover new business opportunities.[3]

The trick, ultimately, is to find the right balance that will allow creativity, competition and communications to maximize a corporation's profits, productivity and competitiveness in the appropriate industries. This is easier said than done. Real synergy opportunities exist in most large companies, but they are rarely as plentiful as executives assume. The challenge is to distinguish the valid opportunities from the mirages. When synergy is well managed, it can be a boon, creating additional value with existing resources. But when it's poorly managed, it can undermine an organization's confidence and erode the trust between business units as well as between the units and the corporate center. Half of the battle when it comes to creating synergy is to have a clear road map of what you want out of your different business units.

BLUEPRINT FOR A NETWORKED FUTURE

For Idei, the blueprint is known as "The Age of Networks". At the annual management conference in May 1997, Idei unfurled Version 1.0 of his blueprint for Sony's future. As he conceived it, Sony's value chain had three major components: electronics, which still is the core business; content (music, movies, computer games); and a critical third link that would assume increasing importance, one that Sony would come to call "network services". This would encompass broadcasting, network distribution and the Internet, and electronic commerce such as home banking and shopping. Integrating and expanding these links in the value chain would enable Sony's "Big Bang", so to speak; the evolution of emergent new business domains. Driven by a parallel explosion in R&D in IT and network technology, these new domains would be the basis of the growth strategy for "the new Sony".

Idei's new Sony is not necessarily a drastic departure from its more familiar path of growth. Rather, it is more of a clear reflection of the results of a slow build-up from decades before. The time has come for the decades of acquisitions of motion pictures, music assets and other preparations to bear fruit. Executives at Sony started planning for diversification well before Idei took the helm, and even before the company considered buying two of America's cultural icons, CBS Records Inc. and Columbia TriStar Pictures, in the late 1980s.

The Betamax setback in the 1970s had sparked a reassessment of some of the fundamental principles that Morita and Ibuka had used to build the company. Sony had a reputation to defend — one of innovation, creativity and a fiery desire to challenge the conventional. This reassessment would change Sony's corporate strategies from the mid 1980s onwards.

In the 1970s, Sony executives decided that the company should no longer hold its hardware innovations close to its chest. Norio Ohga, CEO of Sony Corporation in the 1980s, decided that the company could make money by selling its technology — from chips to miniature video-recording heads — even to its competitors. The company even purchased a small U.S. manufacturer of semiconductor production equipment to bolster its components business.

During that period, there was also the recognition that the key innovations in consumer electronics were increasingly driven by the computer industry (and still are, with the likes of Microsoft entering even the video-game business). After two largely unsuccessful attempts (in the mid 1980s and then a decade later), Sony finally entered the computer field with its VAIO model. It also started a major effort in industrial electronics, making both small video cameras for home use, and some of the early production equipment for high-definition television, which creates images as sharp as those of movies and makes enhanced special effects possible.

The company's third major realization was that, given dwindling profit margins in its core electronics business, it needed to diversify and branch out beyond familiar territory. The Betamax lesson was clearly burnt into the minds of Sony executives who swore that they would never again let what they believed was a technologically inferior rival beat out their product. To guarantee that history didn't repeat itself, Morita believed he needed to own entertainment assets so that he could supply the electronics business with a steady stream of Sony-owned entertainment content. He spent a total of US$7 billion to buy Sony a motion picture studio and a record label.

When Idei became chairman in 1995, he knew that achieving synergies within the diversified portfolio of Sony businesses would be his major challenge. The groundwork had been laid. But how he would change the corporate culture and take a company founded and famous for its analog technology forward into the digital age presented a conundrum. The tradition of innovation and pioneer spirit had to be preserved. But the competition in the digital world had changed the rules of the game, and Sony could no longer run its business units like different companies that just happen to belong under the same parent.

ONLINE BANKING[5]

Sony's new online bank bears a name well-known to consumers, but can consumers really trust it enough to handle their life savings? That's a question that the media posed to Sony when it unveiled SonyBank in June 2001. On the day it was launched, its website was swamped with more than a million visitors, twice the number its computer systems could handle. In its first month, SonyBank landed 21,000 accounts and nearly US$66 million in deposits, exceeding company projections.

The e-bank's debut bodes well for an operation that is an important part of Sony's electronic commerce strategy. Idei has long had the desire to expand further into the realm of information technology. Finance, he believes, fits well with this IT strategy because the data is easily digitized. But a fast start may do little to sustain SonyBank as it runs into stiffer competition and the obstacles that plague online banking everywhere. Most Internet-only banks in other countries are struggling. Analysts say they don't believe that consumers will ever adjust to the idea of managing assets solely online. So SonyBank does run a risk of becoming just another pretty Web interface, rather than a new line of business that fits well with the rest of the company's broadband strategy.

Still SonyBank has a few things going for it. Average consumers are wary of Japan's debt-ridden big banks and may be willing to put aside their qualms about online banks and hand over their nest eggs. With more than US$11 trillion in savings, bonds and other assets, the Japanese are the world's biggest savers. But for decades workers have been expected to place personal accounts with their employer's bank, a practice that spawned a retail banking system that took its customers for granted. Few banks have offered investment or financial management services. Interest rates paid on savings deposits hover near zero.

SonyBank — which is partly owned by U.S. financial-services giant J.P. Morgan and Sumitomo Mitsui Bank — is paying 0.5 per cent interest on time deposits, significantly more than the 0.02–0.05 per cent offered by traditional banks. More importantly, it is offering lower transaction fees, long-term loans, investment trust funds and Web-based financial advice to attract customers. Within five years, SonyBank expects to have 600,000 accounts. Nearly one-third of Japanese households have Internet access, with more than half of all households due to have broadband connection by the end of 2005. SonyBank is targeting younger, Web-savvy customers. "Sony's image is one of reliability," says Masahiro Ono, a Tokyo analyst with brokerage UBS Warburg. "No one has a doubt about Sony."

FIND THE RIGHT MIDDLEMAN

When Idei recently handed Sir Howard Stringer, whom he hired in 1997 as Sony Corporation of America's chief executive, full control of the content and electronics businesses in the U.S., he demonstrated clearly that he was serious about his "Age of Networks". Although Stringer didn't have any operational responsibilities, he was charged with being the coordinator for the content and electronics side of Sony's American operations. Before Stringer, Sony executives said they had been hard-pressed to find an appropriate manager who embodied both an appreciation of Sony's core electronics business and a keen understanding of what it would take to strengthen Sony's then-floundering entertainment businesses. Michael Schulhof, who headed Sony's U.S. operations for almost a decade until 1995, tried, but his misguided attempts to manage the entertainment businesses and bring together the software and hardware sides of Sony were unsuccessful.[6]

One of Idei's biggest challenges in executing his vision was precisely his concern over how to manage Sony's U.S. operations to achieve a subtle balance of influence between the product divisions and the U.S. operations. During the late 1980s, the product divisions had increasingly taken on global responsibility for their products, particularly in the area of development and manufacturing globally. The strategy for product development and manufacturing was largely directed from Tokyo headquarters, a situation which, at times, created tensions between Tokyo and the U.S. operations as to how those operations should be run. Tokyo realized that Sony Corporation of America was an effective marketing and sales organization with an enviable record of long-standing success. No product division could hope to succeed in the U.S. without unqualified support from Sony Corporation of America. With increasingly shorter product cycles and ever-increasing competition, Sony Corporation of America's role continued to become even more important.

The second major challenge was the extent to which the various operations within the U.S. should be integrated. In 1990, integration was limited to Masaaki Morita's serving as chairman for all U.S. hardware operations. Now, however, U.S. entertainment businesses have been organized largely under one umbrella of broadband entertainment. The one exception is Sony Computer Entertainment Inc., which still reports directly to Sony Computer Entertainment in Tokyo. The question then is: What should be the role of Sony Corporation of America in coordinating all of this? Should its role be expanded?

The third challenge, and a very real one today, is how to achieve integration between the company's content and hardware businesses. Technical expertise related to hardware development resided largely in Japan, whereas the center for content development was clearly in the U.S. How much and how fast should management try to promote integration, and how should this be done?

Stringer was Idei's most logical and surest bet to untangle all of these challenges and find a straight path for Sony in the U.S. He had produced the *CBS Evening News with Dan Rather* and *CBS Reports* on his way to becoming the president of CBS News. From 1988 to 1995, he was president of the entire CBS Broadcast Group and was well-connected in the broadcast industry. In 1995, he was lured to head a start-up funded by U.S. telephone providers, the Baby Bells, which experimented with using telephone lines to deliver video into the home.

This eventually folded, but he had acquired experience in new approaches to content distribution. With this background and experience, he would, Idei judged, be an ideal candidate for the role Idei had in mind.

When Stringer first came on board, he didn't enjoy the same kind of independence and autonomy that Schulhof had received when he was chairman. Nor did he really have the kind of control over the electronics side of the business that many would like to think. But, in the five years he has headed Sony's American operations, he has served an even more crucial role coordinating Sony's three operating companies in the U.S. — electronics, entertainment (pictures and music) and computer entertainment. His role, as he sees it, is that of a diplomat. If "synergy" were not such a taboo word within Sony, it would probably be the perfect word to describe what he does.

MEETING HALFWAY: COMMUNICATING WITH ONE ANOTHER[7]

Idei will have none of the hands-off-America policy of his predecessors, who were worried more about cultural and political barriers. He needs the companies, long accustomed to operating separately, to talk to one another (what Stringer calls "connecting the silos" of the operations), to make sure the content providers and the hardware wizards are at least in touch with one another.

Communication has long been a problem area in Sony's attempts to bring closer collaboration between business units. There has long been a cultural gap between the content (entertainment and computer gaming) and the electronics sides of the business. The gap is both cultural in the literal sense — the difference between Japanese and American management styles (in his 1985 memoir, Akio Morita wrote about his disapproval of certain American management styles, such as the over-emphasis on profits over people or the quickness to penalize an employee for a mistake) — and in the divergent natures of the entertainment and electronics industries.

One of Sony's most difficult cultural challenges has been in integrating Columbia TriStar Pictures into its overall portfolio. As we will see in the next chapter, the company's lack of understanding of how Hollywood worked and its inability to manage the executives it put in place at the studios contributed to a considerable financial hemorrhage, which was not staunched until John Calley was put in charge at the studios.

With Stringer at the helm of Sony's U.S. operations and Calley heading the movie business, Sony finally set up a structure that would ensure that the lines of communication between the studios, U.S. headquarters and Tokyo would be open and transparent. It became clear that Idei would only be able to realize a dream of an "Age of Networks" if the networking and communicating started first internally within Sony.

• **Content and technology meetings**

Perhaps the most important avenue of communication when creating synergies is that between the leaders of the individual business units. These unit heads can discuss their concerns, learn from each other, and orchestrate strategies that will benefit the corporation as a whole as well as the individual business units. During the meetings, managers can do a run-through of real-time internal operating numbers and external market statistics. They can also engage in a qualitative discussion of matters of mutual interest — competitors' moves, customer feedback, technology development, and so on.

Within Sony, these content and technology meetings, held periodically in Tokyo, Europe and the U.S., gather chief technology officers from Sony Electronics, Sony Pictures, Sony Music and Sony Computer Entertainment, along with corporate strategists, to discuss how to create common business platforms across the different units. Among the hottest topics under discussion at these meetings recently has been the need to develop digital copyright technology.

Sony engineers, now and throughout the company's history, have been charged with a spirit and mission to be innovative and at the forefront of the technological revolution. One of the recent ways in which they have tried to fulfill this mission was in developing the Net MD, a device that allows consumers to download music from the Internet and store it in a portable Walkman-like device. In principle, this was a great idea and one geared toward the digital world we live in today. But the music side of Sony's business found a problem with this Net MD technology. Within the music industry, one of the biggest challenges facing the record labels is protecting copyright. With websites such as Napster.com and Kazaa.com proliferating, music lovers no longer have to go to record stores to buy CDs, tapes and mini-disks to listen to music by their favorite artists. They just have to go on the Internet and download the songs, most likely for free. (At the time of writing, Napster has declared bankruptcy, and the music industry has brought a lawsuit against Kazaa.) The spread of Internet music players increases the risk for music studios that consumers will trade illegal copies of music, and highlights a conflict between Sony's electronics and content businesses, one tension that could be diminished through more open lines of communication. The electronics and music executives have come together to discuss ways to protect copyright digitally — perhaps using some sort of encryption software to protect online music from being downloaded for free. Sony Music has also allied with other record labels to develop a common policy to handle the downloadable-music trend. But the damage from Napster and other free music sites has already been done. Even though the record labels have proposed for-profit downloadable-music sites, consumers are already so accustomed to the idea of receiving free music from the Internet that it would take a lot of re-education to win public support for fee-based sites.

- **Marketing Strategy Council**

Until recently, if you paid attention to the appliances and devices used in Sony movies, you could see a mixed bag of brands: Hitachi televisions, JVC video cameras, Motorola cell phones, to name but a few. In an age where product placement was the new fad, Sony wasn't taking advantage of it. (Sony Pictures Entertainment executives say that the placement of other brand-named electronic goods was not a result of their purchasing the movie spot, but simply resulted from a lack of coordination.)

But all that has changed in the last two years. With a newly instituted "marketing strategy council", which meets three or four times a year in the U.S., Europe or Tokyo, marketing executives from different Sony divisions and market segments come together to discuss ways to coordinate their campaigns. It provides an opportunity for executives who would not otherwise meet to pool their ideas to compile a more uniform and hard-hitting, brand-building campaign for Sony as a whole. As one executive described it: "The expectation for this marketing council is that we play for the same team and so we should all work together."

Now, as a general rule, Sony Pictures Entertainment makes sure Sony products are used in movies and television shows. For example, instead of an actor holding a Motorola cellular phone, he would be showing off a Sony Ericsson phone. Sony introduced its new color-screen cellular phone during the *Spider-Man* summer blockbuster in 2002. And the Spiderman character has been used to promote a range of Sony products, including Walkmans and computer games.

- **Global Top Meeting**

Every year, Sony's regional heads from around the world gathered in Tokyo to listen to top management describe the corporate vision for the following fiscal year. But to achieve true synergies between the company's content/entertainment and electronics businesses, Sony's top managers believed they needed to have greater coordination and more time to strategize. Hence, the Global Top Meeting. Convened twice a year, it draws together key executives from computer games, movies, music and electronics to exchange views on the global business environment and discuss how Sony's operations can

> "The expectation is that we play for the same team and so we should all work together." — Sony executive

coordinate and prepare for the challenges ahead. The point, one executive explained, is to "make everyone's recognition of the business environment and new opportunities in sync".

For parts of Sony that have largely operated on their own, such as Sony Computer Entertainment, the gradual transition towards a more collaborative corporation has been awkward. But now that it is clear to the industry at large and to Sony executives internally that the PlayStation business will play an increasingly vital role in Sony's revenue stream, it must be brought closer under the parent umbrella, so the synergies with the gaming business can be leveraged elsewhere in the organization.

REDUCE INTER-UNIT COMPETITION

One of the most difficult challenges for large corporations with diversified businesses lies in resolving internal competition. It demands that top management strike a balance between corporate intervention and business-unit autonomy. On the one hand, reducing internal competition and coordinating better responses to cope with mutual competitors could prove to be a powerful and effective way to counter external competition. On the other hand, synergies and collaborations can't be forced. There is usually a good reason when unit managers choose not to cooperate. It maybe that they believe that the costs, including opportunity costs, of collaborating outweigh the benefits. Still, there has to be a mutual understanding and willingness to help one another within the parent corporation.

For Sony, striking this balance between innovating and helping other units has been difficult and a task which, most executives agree, has yet to be fully achieved. In the case of online video games, for example, two Sony units are currently competing in the same market space, independently developing online video-gaming. At Sony Online Entertainment, a subsidiary of Sony Digital Pictures Entertainment, software engineers have developed a game, Everquest, which has gained tremendous popularity among online game players. Everquest has sold a million copies and attracted more than 400,000 online gamers. Sony Online Entertainment also writes games that can be paired for release with movies from the studios, including *Spider-Man* and *Men In Black*. Halfway across the world in Tokyo, another Sony subsidiary, Sony Computer Entertainment, the maker of PlayStation, is scheming to develop an online-gaming platform. The online business is becoming more crucial for PlayStation's survival as the game consoles become more like home appliances for accessing all kinds of interactive entertainment over broadband connections. Although Sony Computer Entertainment used to write little of its gaming software — most are contracted by major third-party game-software engineers such as Square, which developed the Final Fantasy game — this policy is beginning to change. At the same time, Sony Online Entertainment writes some of its own games. The ramifications of having separate development teams for online gaming for both Sony Computer Entertainment and Sony Online Entertainment remain to be seen. One Sony Online Entertainment executive has said that already some of the company's game software is being written with PlayStation in mind, thus demonstrating an effort to create synergies between the different units. But while the separate divisions are pushing forward in the development of an online-gaming community, they will inevitably end up competing with one another for the same business from game players. How Sony will resolve the possible clash between two of its business units is unclear. Since the online-gaming industry is still in its infancy, Sony executives say they are watching its development and the development of broadband usage before making a definitive decision regarding the future of the company's online-gaming activities.

A better example of Sony's efforts to reduce inter-unit competition perhaps would be the discussions over how to resolve concerns on digital copyright, especially for the music industry. The lack of communication between Sony electronics and music units created a clash over the direction of online music distribution. The audio engineers wanted to come up with the best products to meet the needs and expectations of consumers in a digital age. Sony Music, like the rest of the music industry, was watching its profit margins slip with the proliferation of online music. Sony Music worried that Sony's Net MD and other MP3 music format players, such as Apple's IPOD, would likely encourage consumers to move more quickly toward downloadable online music rather than opting to go to the record store to buy an album.

The music industry as a whole was slow to catch on to the demands of the online digital world. Just as record labels resisted when compact-disc technology was introduced and music started moving from tapes to the digital format, they — Sony Music included — were also slow in realizing the burst of popularity in downloadable music. Now, through the various forums instituted by the company, audio engineers and music executives can come together to find ways to resolve any potential clashes.

SHARE TANGIBLE RESOURCES

Up to this point, we've largely discussed the challenges of synergies across units that don't naturally have anything in common. But sometimes even the most obvious synergies can pass unnoticed. Units can sometimes save a lot of money by sharing physical assets or resources. By using a common manufacturing facility or research laboratory, for example, they may gain economies of scale and avoid duplicated effort.

In April 2000, Sony reorganized its various technology centers into Engineering, Manufacturing, and Customer Services systems (EMCs). Before EMCs were introduced, each factory or technology center would act independently for itself. Each would purchase parts that they needed for production. Each factory would be responsible for certain products. But this system didn't allow for flexibility and room to react to changes in the market. For example, if there was a drop in demand for Walkmans or televisions but an increasing demand for Discmans, individual factories producing Walkmans or televisions would see production levels drop. Even though there was less work, the costs of keeping those factories open remained the same. At the same time, factories making Discmans would be overwhelmed by increased demand. Today, instead of organizing factories and production centers around product lines, Sony is organizing them by productivity skills and worker skills. This way, work can be distributed more evenly among the factories. At the same time, the purchasing of parts for the products is more centralized, reducing build-ups or shortages of stock.

CO-EVOLVING: MAKING SYNERGIES WORK

The jury is still out on how the diversification into music, gaming and movies has actually benefited Sony. The computer-games business has been the only area that has brought in steady revenues. The music business and the movie business have not found the kind of synergies with the rest of the corporate family that executives had hoped for. At the core, Sony was and still remains a consumer-electronics company — even as that sector continues to sink in economic quicksand. With each passing year, industry's overstocked supply chain is reducing Sony's new models of MP3 players, Handycams, CD players and cell phones to rank commodities. The Sonys, Sanyos and Samsungs of the world all have access to the same huge pool of chips, liquid-crystal displays, audio pickups, power supplies and packaging as the Chinese upstarts. To see what impact this has had on prices, you need look no further than the DVD market, where Sony once ruled the roost. Now, some of the hottest models are Chinese DVD players selling for less than US$100.

It is absolutely crucial for Sony to find the right synergies between its business units to leverage a more encompassing strategy for coping with the digital broadband world. Sony's rivals are no longer simply fellow manufacturers of consumer electronics: they now span the computing industry, the entertainment industry, the media conglomerates and many others. To survive in the digital world, as Nobuyuki Idei sees it, Sony employees have to become digital dream kids, thinking in ways that will help network the company's different resources. But as the next chapter will show, finding the right balance between different corporate cultures, management styles and industries is a major challenge.

SONY'S RECIPES FOR SUCCESS

- *Understand why you need to create synergies*: Often companies force synergies between business units that don't have common ground on which to collaborate. Forcing synergies can often undermine the original successes of individual groups and take away their competitive advantages against outside rivals without offering them new competitive edges.

- *Recognize your strengths*: To find synergies between your business units, you have to first understand the respective strengths of your business units. This will give a clearer picture of how well their different strategies will fit with one another.

- *Communicate well*: The surest way for synergies to fail is through a lack of communication. Sometimes units are accustomed to being independent, working autonomously from the parent company. To ask these units to suddenly work together, collaborate, can sometimes to be a tough challenge. And the only way to establish common ground between business units is through good communication.

- *Reduce inter-unit competition*: In corporations with a diverse business portfolio, you often find business units that compete with one another for consumers or directly affect each other's business. It is vital that the parent company finds a way for these business units to reduce internal competition that could undermine the company's overall business strategy.

- *Share tangible resources*: Part of the benefit of creating synergies is a reduction in costs. Business units may often be able to share common facilities such as factory space, supplies or marketing resources. By finding where resources overlap and sharing them, corporations can find higher efficiency and more cost savings.

NOTES

1. Kathleen M. Eisenhardt and D. Charles Galunic, "Coevolving: At Last, A Way to Make Synergies Work", *Harvard Business Review*, January-February, 2000, pp. 91–101.

2. David E. Sanger, "Why Sony Stalked Columbia? Demand for Entertainment Soars", *New York Times*, September 28, 1989.

3. Michael Gould and Andrew Campbell, "Desperately Seeking Synergy", *Harvard Business Review*, September–October, 1998, pp.131–143.

4. Sony corporate website, www.sony.net.

5. Mutsuko Murakami, "Can A Brand Be A Bank?", *Asiaweek*, August 10, 2001.

6. Nathan, op. cit.

Information in this section is drawn from interviews with Sony Pictures executives Susan Tick, Takehito Soeda, Don Levy and others.

Six

QUITTERS NEVER WIN: ACQUIRING COLUMBIA TRISTAR PICTURES

In 1989 Sony paid $3.4 billion for Columbia TriStar Pictures, a move that Akio Morita believed would give Sony a competitive advantage because it now had the content to feed its electronics products. Instead, Sony found itself spending an exorbitant amount of money for a studio and managers who produced a string of box office bombs that forced it to announce losses in its movies division in late 1994. The synergies that Morita had expected have still to be fully realized. But Sony never turned its back on the movie project, and now, Sony Pictures Entertainment appears to be turning things around. This chapter documents the Sony Pictures story and the lessons Sony learned about synergizing.

When it comes to creating synergy, sometimes even the best of companies fail. What distinguishes the best from the rest is the way they handle the setback. Much of how this unfolds is a reflection of the corporation's values and culture.

In 1989, when Sony paid US$3.4 billion for Columbia TriStar Pictures, industry observers largely mocked the company for paying over the odds for a studio that was already struggling financially. Then Sony paid several hundred million more to lure managers away from Warner Brothers, provoking a costly legal battle in the process. Those managers, in turn, spent money extravagantly and produced a string of box office bombs, forcing Sony in late 1994 to announce losses in its movies division. For Akio Morita, the string of problems that arose from his acquisition of Columbia Pictures was a truly disappointing outcome to his dream of owning a movie studio.

The Columbia Pictures acquisition was one of Sony's most scrutinized deals and the subsequent turbulence it caused almost certainly took the company by surprise. Just two years before, Sony had completed its first American acquisition, the purchase of CBS Records for $2 billion, to add breadth and depth to its business. Despite some criticism, the CBS Records acquisition was largely smooth. So following that with a bid for a movie studio seemed a natural and logical next step for Sony, which was looking to diversify and acquire content to complement its hardware electronic gadgets.

But despite the subsequent hemorrhaging of profits and perhaps, even more importantly, the disappointment Sony's top executives must have had over the acquisition of Columbia Pictures, the company never turned its back on the movie project. It just kept trying to reinvent, refine and challenge itself to accomplish what outside observers thought would never be possible: In 2002, with blockbusters such as *Spider-Man* and sequel successes such as *Stuart Little 2* and *Men In Black II*, the studio (renamed Sony Pictures Entertainment in 1991) enjoyed a banner summer and showed prospects that 2002 could become the studio's second profitable year since coming under Sony's management.

At a strategy meeting in New York in May 2002, Nobuyuki Idei, chairman of Sony Corp., opened the meeting with an exclamation: "Did you see our *Spider-Man* movie?" Like proud parents showing off their newborn child, Sony executives could now finally brag about their acquisition to others.

MATCHMAKING: GETTING HARDWARE AND SOFTWARE TOGETHER

Sony Pictures turned in a report card with all 'A's for 2002, with the string of blockbusters bringing in much-needed revenues for the studio. But the challenge of fully integrating the studio into the Sony group still looms over the company. After Sony's first hand-picked studio executives exhausted the studio's resources, the company brought in new management in 1996, revamping how the studio handled costs. Now, what remains to be done is the most important step in the synergy process: merging corporate cultures. Capturing cross-business synergies is at the heart of corporate strategy these days — the promise of synergy is a prime rationale for the existence of the multi-business corporation.

For Sony, the acquisition of Columbia TriStar Pictures was supposed to complement the company's line of electronic gadgets.

After getting burned in the Betamax saga in the 1970s, Sony had concluded that control of software or programming might give it an edge as it introduced new hardware technology. "If I owned a movie studio, Betamax would not have come out second best," Akio Morita is reported to have told Walter Yetnikoff, president and chief executive officer of CBS Records at the time. Sony executives, particularly Morita, believed that Sony might have prevailed if it had been able to put out a stream of its own popular movies in the Betamax format.

Although Sony rebounded quickly from the Betamax fiasco, the episode was one that Sony would never forget. Morita believed that Sony now needed to diversify beyond the fickle consumer-electronics business. Industry observers and analysts agreed. It was becoming hard to keep "living from magic show to magic show", as *Fortune* magazine put it.[1] Profit margins from consumer-electronics products were beginning to get slimmer and slimmer with the standardization of technology. Sony was no longer able to go on inventing new products that nobody knew they needed and then watch as competitors came up with cheaper imitations.

Sony pressed ahead with measures designed to diversify its activities. Instead of looking to consumer products to generate 80 per cent of its business, it pursued a "50–50 strategy", aiming to sell less to consumers and more to businesses. It broke with its own tradition by selling components to other manufacturers, plunged into workstation computers, and built its own semiconductor facilities.

But another notion was burned into Morita's consciousness: If you control the content, the public will have to accept your hardware. Morita, who had been so deeply impressed by the Dutch electronics giant Royal Philips Electronics when he first visited in the late 1950s, once again gazed upon that company with a jealous eye. Philips owned PolyGram Records, which, Morita believed, helped its compact disc sales. In 1986, Sony was developing the digital tape recorder. Linking the new technology with the world's largest record company might make the new recorder much more attractive to consumers. Though the digital audio technology, overshadowed by the compact disc, never caught on, the underlying thinking was what prompted Sony to buy CBS Records Inc. and to start patrolling for a movie studio.[2]

SETTING A PRECEDENT

CBS Records was the first major Japanese purchase of an American company — and CBS Records was a particularly American company. Originally the Columbia Phonograph Company, its first stars were John Philip Sousa and the U.S. Marine Band. CBS was virtually an All-American record label. Under its label were some of America's most renowned artists spanning a broad spectrum of genres: Duke Ellington and Bessie Smith; Bob Dylan and Bruce Springsteen; Michael Jackson and Barbra Streisand were all under its management. It recorded classic musicals from *My Fair Lady* to *A Chorus Line*. Naturally, there were some in the music industry who expressed concern about the implications of Japanese ownership of what they considered an American icon.

In the first reports of the deal, analysts concluded that the price was too high. Even Yetnikoff warned Morita and the then-president of Sony, Norio Ohga, that this was the case. But the deal eventually proved to be brilliant — so much so that when Sony subsequently decided to buy a movie company, it hardly worried when the same critics again said it was paying too much.[3]

SHARE THE BURDEN, WORK WITH OTHERS

Sometimes successful corporations believe they can go into new markets alone, without help. But working with partners that already have the expertise in those markets can expedite entry. Combine your ambitions with a partner's know-how, and you are more likely to produce an effective and successful business plan.

The Sony-CBS Records marriage was a smooth arrangement. But that really wasn't a surprise given that the two companies had a history of working together. The two companies had set up a joint venture in Japan in the late 1960s. There had been clashes along the way, of course, as is to be expected in any business partnership. The biggest of these clashes was over home taping of audio recordings. CBS contended that Sony was creating taping technology that harmed its record business by allowing consumers to make free copies of records at home. (Sony Electronics and Sony Music now have similar conflicts over downloadable music and how to protect copyrights.) But in spite of these bumps along the way, the Sony-CBS joint venture was relatively smooth and uneventful. As part of its typical practice with overseas assets, when Sony acquired CBS Records in the U.S. it retained most of the existing management.

The smooth transition of the CBS acquisition gave Sony a big boost of confidence when it made a bid for Columbia Pictures. But, as it turns out, the Columbia acquisition would not turn out to be as neat and tidy as Sony had presumed.

WHY SONY AND CBS GOT TOGETHER IN THE FIRST PLACE[4]

At the beginning of the 1960s, trade friction between Japan and the rest of the world was growing. While its shipbuilding, textile and other industries were rapidly increasing their exports, Japan maintained strict restrictions on imports and foreign-exchange transactions, citing balance of payments worries as justification. Facing pressure from its trading partners to remove restrictions, the Japanese government gradually began to ease tariff and foreign exchange limitations. With deregulation in progress, foreign companies were allowed to set up subsidiaries or joint ventures in Japan, acquire equity stakes in Japanese companies and participate in the management of these companies.

At the time, CBS was very interested in expanding its music business into Japan and was looking for a partner to set up a subsidiary there. CBS Records commanded a 20 per cent share of the worldwide record market, and it boasted technological developments that included the LP record. Although CBS Records had been supplying Japan Columbia Inc. with vinyl discs for many years, the two companies could not come to an agreement on a joint venture.

In the summer of 1967, Harvey Schein (then president of CBS International and later president of Sony Corporation of America) visited Japan to talk to various record companies. However, while all of them listened earnestly to Schein's plans, none of them would give him a straight answer with regard to setting up a joint venture. In October of that year, after several frustrating months trying to find a partner, Schein thought of Akio Morita, then Sony's executive deputy president, whom he knew through Sony's broadcast equipment business. Schein approached Morita merely to ask for advice regarding his proposal. He hadn't expected Morita to turn around and ask him "How about setting up a joint venture with Sony?"

After months of non-commitment from other Japanese companies, Schein was a bit taken aback by the speed with which Morita proposed the venture. A year later, CBS Sony Records Inc. was born. Capitalized at ¥720 million, it was the first foreign–Japanese joint venture to be set up in the wake of Japan's capital deregulation. Morita was quick to agree to the venture because he believed that it would establish Sony as a major worldwide manufacturer of both hardware and music software.

THE COLUMBIA TRISTAR PICTURES STORY

As with the announcement of the acquisition of CBS Records, news of Sony's acquisition of Columbia TriStar was greeted with an outcry over the sale of a venerated and uniquely American institution to a foreign acquirer. This time it was exacerbated by a wave of Japanese companies snapping up American properties, from the Rockefeller Center in New York to the rolling resorts of Hawaii. This was the 1980s, and Japan was experiencing an incredible economic boom.

Companies had cash to spare and started looking abroad for outlets on which to spend the money. Although Sony was seen as something of a brash upstart at home, it was viewed by many in the United States as part of this rich and invincible army of foreign invaders. The fact that Sony was willing to meet a price of more than US$5 billion (counting the debt it agreed to carry for Columbia TriStar) only inflamed American anxieties. (Columbia TriStar was actually not Sony's first choice. The studio, then owned by Coca-Cola, was in bad financial shape. Morita had long admired MCA/Universal, but its owner, Lew Wasserman, wasn't keen to sell. During the summer of 1988, after Sony's executives met with heads of the studios, it became clear that only MGM and Columbia were possibilities. MGM's demands quickly eliminated it as a possibility, leaving Sony with only Columbia Pictures to consider. Despite the financial difficulties of the studio, it was the only major studio to have retained rights to its entire library of films, 2,700 titles, which became an appealing selling point for Sony.)[5]

Sony expressed its regret over American reaction to the deal. But it didn't concern itself too much with criticism that it had paid too much, criticism it had heard before about its overspending on CBS Records, which had proven to be a false alarm. Having made one successful foray into the entertainment world, Sony had every reason to think it could win again in the movie business.

Sony was hardly the first company to fall into the Hollywood trap. The movie business has long attracted an array of hopeful outsiders, from insurance companies to soft-drinks giants. Many have learned the hard way that Hollywood is a world apart — a risky industry where the uninitiated are routinely shorn. It is very much a fantasy factory where insiders are often more skilled at creating illusions about themselves than they are at spinning magic for the big screen. Sony would soon find all of this out the hard way.

LOCALIZATION: THE ILLUSIONS OF DREAM-TEAM MANAGEMENT

The American managers of Sony knew that Morita would not go with a motion pictures acquisition without knowing the candidates the company could get to run the show. As discussed earlier, Sony has long had an unspoken policy of using local talent to run local operations. It was part of Morita's belief in global localization. In both Europe and the U.S., that strategy had proven quite successful, particularly in negotiations with local governments. After all, local talent typically meant local expertise and connections within the country's business community. Columbia Pictures was no exception — it was, in fact, far more crucial for Sony to trust and depend on the managers they would handpick to run the show. Hollywood was a very different beast from Sony's usual business environment. For starters, the managers at Sony knew very little about the techniques and technicalities of movie making or what it takes to make a hit movie that would bring in the revenues. Neither did Tokyo-based executives have the necessary network of contacts to sign on the big stars to make the studio profitable. So despite Morita's desperate desire to own a motion pictures business and achieve the synergies he envisioned, he was adamant about finding the right talent.

Finding suitable managers with the brains, guts and instincts to run a Hollywood studio has always been difficult. The job calls for individuals who can make constant decisions involving hundreds of millions of dollars. Business sense isn't enough;

a studio chief needs to have some intuition about what will entertain the fickle public and some rapport with temperamental actors and directors. With a fickle audience, the studio manager needed to understand how to manipulate the movie industry, select the right films and market them into becoming the blockbusters that would bring in the revenues. Indecision could not be tolerated: the distribution system was a gaping maw that needed to be filled constantly with one picture after another.

Aside from movies, there were also television operations, home video and theaters. Overheads typically roared along at more than US$100 million a year. Failures were highly publicized.

As a result, the few who demonstrated an ability to achieve consistent success were jealously guarded by their employers and given handsome long-term contracts. Sony's chief negotiators, CBS chairman and long-time Sony friend Walter Yetnikoff and Sony Corporation of American chief executive Michael Schulhof, knew very well that these A-list people weren't likely to jump ship to Sony's newly acquired studio, especially considering the stigma at the time involved in going to work for the first Japanese owner of a Hollywood studio.

On paper, Peter Guber and Jon Peters, the two producers tapped to run Columbia Pictures for Sony, gave the impression of being genuine movie moguls. They were, after all, high-profile producers who had just made *Batman*, the largest grossing film at the time, for the Warner Brothers Studio. In their production resume were such hits as *Rain Man* and *The Color Purple*. But the real players in Hollywood knew that Guber and Peters were not hands-on filmmakers.

For example, when Stephen Spielberg made *The Color Purple*, he had a provision in his contract explicitly barring them from the set. Observers say Guber and Peters may have seemed an impressive pair, but their greatest gift was actually for promotion — especially self-promotion. What was lacking was any credential or experience that would qualify them to run a major studio.

BALANCING ACT: HIRE LOCALLY BUT COMMUNICATE OFTEN

It is important to hire people who have a keen understanding of the new markets your company is expanding toward. But there is a delicate balancing act between giving these expert managers autonomy to develop the new business and maintaining some sort of control over their decisions. The key to achieving this balance is communication. Always keep the lines of communication between the headquarters and the new business units open, and don't be afraid to ask managers to explain to you the new markets and the strategies they plan to embark on. After all, it's your company.

Guber and Peters were renowned for their aggression. Hollywood observers described them rather unkindly as grabbers who snatched material, credit and money, leaving a swath of dazed victims in their wake. It was a management style that Sony executives — coming from a Japanese tradition of teamwork and long-term commitments to their firms — could hardly be expected to grasp, but would soon learn about the hard way. But Sony executives, not understanding the history of Hollywood or the people involved, could not have known this at the time.

There was no doubt that Hollywood insiders were surprised at Sony's hiring of Guber and Peters, but perhaps they were more stunned by how much Sony had agreed to pay for the services of two amateur studio executives. In addition to buying Guber and Peters' loss-making production company for $200 million — about 40 per cent higher than its market value — Sony also offered the two a rich compensation package that included $2.75 million each in annual salary (not including hefty annual bonuses), a $50-million bonus pool, and a stake in any increase in the studio's value over the ensuing five years.

As soon as the ink on the deal was dry, Warner slapped Sony with a billion-dollar lawsuit. Guber and Peters had just signed a generous contract with that studio before agreeing to come to Columbia TriStar Pictures, but Sony had failed to review the agreement when it negotiated with them. Sony had known from the start that Peters and Guber were under contract to Warner and had pushed for a definite answer on whether they would be released from their contract. At the time, Peters and Guber said that they had a long-standing oral agreement that Warner executives would release them from their five-year deal. Perhaps it was the way that the announcement was handled — Steve Ross, the head of Warner Bros., heard second hand that Peters and Guber were planning to make a break for Sony — that exacerbated matters and led directly to Warner's legal challenge to Sony's claim on Guber and Peters.

Forced into a settlement worth as much as $800 million, Sony suddenly found the expenses of hiring Guber and Peters had shot up dramatically. Many in the movie business suspected that Sony's nightmare was only beginning. For five years, Sony executives in Tokyo and New York would stand by as the studio lost billions and became a symbol for the worst kind of excess in an industry that is hardly known for moderation. From 1989 until late 1994, during Guber and Peters' reign over Sony's Hollywood studio, the company would only see box-office bombs, lavish renovations, and extravagant parties, all giving outside observers reasons to point fingers and smirk about Sony's single most publicized failure. When Sony finally stepped in to clean up the mess, it would shell out another exorbitant amount of money to fire Guber and Peters, who left the studio without having made a hit and with few movies the pipeline.

The wake-up call for Sony sounded in late 1993. Morita, the 72-year-old chairman and the orchestrator behind Sony's entertainment acquisitions, was playing tennis one Tuesday morning at the end of November when he complained of feeling dizzy. He went home and then, feeling no better, went by ambulance to the Tokyo Medical and Dental University Hospital. As it turned out, he had had a stroke, one from which he would never entirely recover.

Morita's illness immediately sharpened the focus on the questions about Sony's future. Any tangible synergy from the expensive acquisition of Columbia Pictures had still not materialized after four years. Although Sony's U.S. chief, Schulhof, had labored to bring about synergies, holding "opportunities meetings" involving various hardware and software divisions, Sony synergy was still more hope than reality. During Guber and Peters' tenure, Sony Pictures had never produced a genuine breakaway hit. Nor did Columbia Pictures boast any high-profile film for the upcoming Christmas holidays when Guber was finally asked to resign in 1994. At that point, TriStar, the sister division, hadn't put a film into production for nearly a year.

In November 1994, Sony stunned Hollywood and Wall Street by announcing that it was taking a $3.2 billion loss in its second quarter because of its failures in Hollywood. The write-off — essentially a clearing of the balance sheet, which included a $2.7 billion loss on the studio and an additional $510 million operating loss on "settlement of outstanding lawsuits and contract claims" — was one of the largest losses in Japanese corporate history. It was also one of the worst beatings ever sustained by a foreign investor in an American company. After putting on a happy public face for half a decade, Sony was admitting that its foray into Hollywood had been a disaster.

But it wasn't about to give up.

BELIEVING: PART OF THE WINNING FORMULA

Some have said that the reason Sony stuck by Columbia Pictures for so long was that it couldn't find a buyer for a studio that was hemorrhaging money and had no hit movies in sight. Critics could be forgiven for having a jab at Sony for signing up for something it just didn't understand. Although the Columbia TriStar Pictures acquisition did prove to be a big pothole in Sony's road to diversification, the fact that it has stood steadfastly by the business unit through its hard times makes the acquisition an appropriate case study to illustrate aspects of Sony's corporate culture, of its "never give up" spirit and of its ambitions to become more than a consumer-electronics giant. For the year 2002, at least, it seems like the story might have a fairy-tale ending after all.

Immediately after the Guber/Peters era, Sony Pictures Entertainment got little in the way of a break. Sony's holiday slate for 1996 began disappointingly in November with *The Mirror Has Two Faces*. Hopes had been high for this Barbra Streisand movie, which during previews had scored higher than *Sleepless in Seattle*. But critics lambasted Barbra and her narcissism and the film's muddled message. She bathed herself in vanity lighting and underwent a beautifying makeover, all the while ostensibly pushing the theme that looks aren't important.

But Sony did finally find the American managers it needed to run a studio professionally, effectively and successfully. The top job at Columbia Pictures went to United Artists president John Calley, a 66-year-old entertainment-industry veteran. A former Warner executive, Calley had decided in 1980 that he wanted to leave the entertainment industry, turning down a 17-year, $21-million contract. Tired of being "defined by my phone list", Calley retreated to Fishers Island in New York, and stayed out of the movie business until 1989, when he became Mike Nichols' partner, producing Sony releases *Postcards from the Edge* and *The Remains of the Day*. In 1993, he was hired to revive Metro Goldwyn Mayer's dormant United Artists label. There, he enjoyed solid successes such as *Goldeneye* and *The Birdcage*, although he also suffered through losers including *Wild Bill* and *Tank Girl*.

When he returned to Hollywood, Calley had said explicitly that he was planning to stay for only a few years. Given those comments and the extent of the financial problems at Sony's movie studio, many executives and analysts were surprised he said yes to the Sony job. Many quickly jumped to the conclusion that he must have been hired to clean up the studio and prepare it for sale. After all, Calley had helped fatten up MGM/UA, which had just been auctioned off. But then-president Nobuyuki Idei promptly repeated the company line that Sony had no intention of selling, but would try to take the studio public in the next few years.

Internally, Calley's hiring was well received. He was a respected and sophisticated man whose presence as chief would — if nothing else — help burnish Sony's sadly tarnished reputation.

A NEW START[6]

With Calley, Sony was determined to get the management combination right. Instead of adopting a hands-off approach as they had with Peters and Guber, Sony headquarters restructured the chain of command at Sony Pictures Entertainment. Calley would report to Idei, tightening the link between Tokyo and Hollywood. And, for the first time, a Japanese was added to the management mix at the studio. Idei brought in electronics executive Masayuki Nozoe to serve as the liaison between the studio and headquarters in Tokyo. The old laissez-faire days appeared to be over. "This team represents a new vision and direction for the studio," Idei said at the time. On the Culver City lot of Sony Pictures Entertainment, there was exultation over news of Calley's appointment. A basket of flowers, a gift from a staffer, greeted Calley when he reported for his first day of work at the Thalberg Building's Louis B. Mayer Suite. "Help us, Obi-Wan Kenobi," the card read; "You're our only hope."

By Christmas season 1996, there seemed to be some hope. *Jerry Maguire* had a smashing $17-million opening in December, and quickly became the success story of the season, embraced by audiences and critics alike. It would be the only picture turned out by a major studio to be nominated for best picture the following year. (The other nominees — *Shine*, *The English Patient*, *Fargo*, and *Secrets and Lies* — all came from independents.) In all, *Jerry Maguire* received five nominations in plum categories, including Cruise's best-actor nomination and Cuba Gooding, Jr.'s for best supporting actor. (Only Gooding Jr. won.) Even with *Jerry Maguire*'s success, the studio would finish that year in fifth place among the major studios, with only 10.4 per cent market share. It was clear to all that the studio and its new leader, Calley, faced monumental challenges ahead.

> "The acquisition was not just an asset to hold on to. It was meant to become integrated as part of the Sony family."
> — Sony executive

But the words "not giving up" rang true with Sony's attitude toward its motion picture acquisition. As one Sony Pictures executive described it, "the acquisition was not just an asset to hold onto. It was meant to become integrated as part of the Sony family." In response to a controversial book, *Hit and Run: How Jon Peters and Peter Guber Took Sony for a Ride in Hollywood*, the inside story of Sony's acquisition of Columbia Pictures, then-chairman Norio Ohga said: "We will never give up or dispose of Sony Pictures. Even though many people say that the management of the software industry is very difficult, unless you can manage it properly I think the company cannot survive the twenty-first century."

A LEANER, MEANER MACHINE

With the extravagant spending days over and new management in place, Sony Pictures Entertainment got rid of some of its old policies on movie line-ups and tried a different tack to capture new market share and show its might in the Hollywood scene. It was obvious to almost everyone that hits had been rare since Sony bought the studio in 1989, and that was the first thing that needed to be fixed. When Calley came into office, he brought in a team of Hollywood veterans, people who had a proven record in the movie business. First, he promoted long-undervalued executive Garreth Wigan to a more senior role. He also hired Sony alumna Amy Pascal, the well-regarded president of the newly defunct Turner Pictures, as president of Columbia Pictures. Now Calley, with an experienced and trustworthy team, was ready to take on the challenges of running the long-neglected studio.

Calley had three major priorities: cutting costs, developing a better slate of potential hit movies, and forming closer connections with the rest of Sony.

- **Keep costs low**

In 2000, after suffering losses two years in a row, Sony reversed its long-held policy of not sharing costs with other studios in making its movies. The previous logic had been to take total control of the film and milk it for whatever technology might be developed to exploit it. No more. To begin with, Sony bought half the rights to Universal Studio's hit *Erin Brockovich* and also had a half-interest in Dreamworks SKG's '70s rock film *Almost Famous*, a critical hit but lackluster at the box office. It also bought a half-interest in Schwarzenegger's *The 6th Day*.

Sony's new attitude toward sharing the costs was only part of a financial overhaul that began in the late 1990s after Calley took over. Since then, Sony has eliminated its fledgling family-film unit, merged its TriStar film label into Columbia, and ended several pricey deals with producers. And in a recent standoff with director Michael Mann, it refused to make the Will Smith boxing film, *Ali*, until the director slashed costs and agreed to help cover any overruns of its $106-million budget. It also shared production costs with Germany's Initial Entertainment Group.

The most dramatic change at Sony, however, was its sweeping six-year deal with former Walt Disney Studios chairman Joe Roth. Under this agreement, Sony pays half the costs of as many as eight films a year, effectively turning over to Roth the control of one-third of the movies it releases. This will undoubtedly prove to be quite costly, given Roth's track record of working with top-flight stars like Julia Roberts and Bruce Willis.

Potential cost savings aside, why would a corporation like Sony, which guards its assets closely, give up so much control? According to Calley, the studio gets more time to focus on the 15 or so films that aren't being made by outsiders. Idei puts it more simply: "We make too many pictures."

As part of a global cost-cutting effort, Sony Pictures Entertainment slashed a total of $150 million in overheads, particularly scaling back network television production. Unlike in the past, television is no longer a profit-making proposition unless it is syndicated by the networks. "What we've realized is that the market share for cable and network television has changed," says one Sony Pictures

Entertainment executive. (Sony is prohibited from acquiring a cable-television network because it is a foreign-owned company.) Cable television is now getting a lot more attention than it used to, and the profits from making network shows are dwindling, unless, of course, the show is syndicated. Sony has said it will no longer develop television shows for the U.S. audience. Under the Sony Pictures Entertainment banner, television shows such as *Mad About You, Seinfeld* and *The King of Queens* were produced.

In the weekend that *Spider-Man* premiered in Summer 2002, it racked up more than $114 million in U.S. ticket sales — more, even, than the $90.3 million first-weekend gross achieved by *Harry Potter and the Sorcerer's Stone* the year before. The turnaround for Sony underscores Hollywood's fickle nature: Studios can be on top one year and be buried the next. Sony has had a few hits over the years, but nothing like this. Though it must prove that it has box-office staying power, its sudden success earns the studio new cachet in Japan: Sony says that its Hollywood assets are now worth at least $14 billion.

- **A better slate of movies**

For Calley and his team, this success has been long awaited, after they struggled to follow through on projects left behind by the previous regime and to formulate a new strategy. It was years in the making, but soon the studio buzz was all about a slate of sure-bet films for summer 2002. "It's all about putting a program together," Amy Pascal said, defending the time it took to turn things around. The deals for *Spider-Man* and the sequel to *Men In Black* were more difficult to put together than the movies themselves, she added. Launching a slate of blockbusters has sent a powerful signal to Hollywood — and

Wall Street — that Sony Pictures is determined to be a survivor. But it has also been an expensive gamble, costing nearly $600 million in film production alone. That is as much as some studios, including Sony, spend in a year.

What has Sony done differently with its slate of movies? For one thing, the lineup is more varied. There are more film franchises and closer ties to actors. This new strategy started to take place in the late 1990s, a few years after the new Calley management team settled in. Film franchising means making it big on sequels such as *Men In Black II*, *Stuart Little 2*, and now *Spider-Man* and *Charlie's Angels*, which both have sequels.

These sequels, building on hits, secure the studio at least a few successful films a year that bring in the much-needed flow of revenues. To secure franchise talent, in 2000 Sony cemented multi-film deals with superstars like Drew Barrymore, Adam Sandler, Jennifer Lopez and Will Smith. Adam Sandler's Happy Madison Production Company has its offices located on Sony Pictures Entertainment's Culver City studio lots.

The slate of movies is also aiming to appeal to a larger audience demographic. "I wanted to buy things I loved, but they also had to pass the 'Friday-night test'," said Pascal, the executive in charge of selecting movies for Sony. "That means [even] if you had a lousy week, have to pay a baby sitter or take a bus, you were going to go see that movie. Before, I was making movies that I love, but did not have that sense of urgency."

- **Searching for synergies**

When Sony's summer blockbuster, *Spider-Man*, premiered in 2002, Sony Ericsson quickly partnered with U.S. wireless-phone provider Cingular to market a Sony Ericsson phone with a Spiderman face. With blue and red and a Spiderman image on the cover, the T61z Sony Ericsson phone made its debut in the U.S., and became the first Sony Ericsson/Sony Pictures collaborative marketing effort in the U.S. As Bo Larson, corporate vice-president and general manager for Sony Ericsson North America, commented during the launch, the *Spider-Man* program leverages Sony's entertainment strengths with complementary Sony products.

SONY DIGITAL ENTERTAINMENT[7]

Of all the Sony companies, Sony Digital Entertainment, a subsidiary of Sony Pictures Entertainment, is probably the most synergized unit of the group. Its businesses rely on all the different parts of Sony to work together. Within Sony Digital Entertainment, there is Imageworks, which is charged with digital character animation and console-game development. Within the past year (2002), the unit has worked with the U.S. military to apply Hollywood technology to create combat-simulation games. Ultimately, though, the games developed will be targeted for PlayStation, which doesn't develop many of its own. Sony Online Entertainment develops online games, including Everquest, one of the most popular games in the U.S. It also works with Sony Pictures Entertainment to develop online extensions of popular television game shows shows such as *Jeopardy* and *Wheel of Fortune*. Sony Digital Entertainment Digital Networks develops software such as Soapcity and Screenblast. Screenblast allows users to produce their own music, video and animation. The software can connect to Sony digital cameras as well as those from other companies. "As a company, we may want to serve a company's every need, but we understand that consumers buy different components," says one Sony Digital Entertainment Executive. "It would be great if they had all Sony products and Sony devices. But that's just not realistic."

Perhaps the most crucial synergy-creating unit of Sony Digital Pictures Entertainment is its Advanced Platform Group, which is plugged in with Sony's research and development teams in Tokyo and San Jose to see what technology is coming up so that the company can develop services to complement the products. For example, Movielink, a joint venture between five motion-picture studios to allow people to watch movies online, is coordinated with Sony Electronics so that consumers with Sony computers, cellular phones, networked televisions and Cliés have compatible systems to download the movies from the Movielink software.

This is the new age of Sony synergies — and the real reason Sony bought Columbia Pictures to start with. As mentioned earlier, the thinking at the time of the acquisition was that Columbia Pictures, with its movies, television shows and library of video tapes (and now DVDs), would complement Sony's existing strengths in electronics, such as the VAIO computer and the Vega television theater system, and make the entire Sony package a whole lot more attractive. Until recently, it hadn't been very clear exactly how Sony movies have added value to the Sony brand. Sony movies still carry the Columbia Pictures icon, the woman in a toga holding a torch aloft. Computers, cellular phones and other electronic devices used in the movies are not necessarily Sony products. The synergies that Morita had envisioned would happen, haven't been realized yet.

Achieving the most superficial synergies within the Sony group really shouldn't be difficult, as we discussed in the previous chapter. The simplest way is product placement — using Sony products in Sony movies. Sony Pictures Entertainment officials admit that, until the past year or so, there has been no standing policy or coordination within the Sony group to ensure that Sony products are used in Sony movies and television shows. Sony Ericsson phones will now feature ring tones from Sony movie themes such as *Spider-Man* and *Men In Black II*, and screen savers on the phones will also feature Sony Pictures' characters.

ONLINE MOVIES[8]

In an attempt to avoid the digital copyright issues which plague the music industry , movie studios are trying to pre-empt the onslaught of downloadable movies by introducing their own online-movie ventures in hopes to entice consumers to pay for something before they can get it for free illegally.

Traditionally, the entertainment industry has fought such new devices, on the grounds that they threaten copyrights, before reluctantly accepting them. Now the industry is pushing a new wave of innovations — digital-rights technology, paid Internet services and a standardized method of delivering digital signals across platforms — to pave the way for the expected explosion in online videos and movies. There is no doubt that the music industry's dwindling profits in record-album sales and the proliferation of illegal, free music-sharing sites have served as wake-up calls to the movie studios to take action before it's too late.

As Walt Disney Co., Sony Pictures Entertainment and several other studios join forces and prepare to roll out online movie services this year, a tug-of-war is playing out between advocates of new technology designed to give consumers unprecedented access to movies and music, and the entertainment industry's new technology aimed at imposing restrictions on how consumers use the products. But the market in for-profit online-video services is far from certain.

A formidable consumer faction has grown accustomed to getting movies and music free from Morpheus and the old Napster. In addition, the Justice Department is investigating the studios' alliances for possible antitrust violations.

The greatest potential obstacle to the success of an online video venture is whether it will make money. One revenue source, though serving mainly as an insurance policy to prevent erosion of their bottom line from Napster-like services, is the licensing of the content. While they can't completely wipe out piracy, studios are working aggressively to shore up what they see as gaps in the copyright law to prevent the loss of millions of dollars from unauthorized duplication.

Already, software companies such as Microsoft and some law firms are offering digital-rights management systems that set the rules and parameters for how content will be licensed and used over digital media. The services provide encryption and water-marking as well as tracing capabilities to help the media companies protect their digital assets. But the media giants want to go even further to set industry-wide standards on how their content can and can't be used. With no road map to follow in this largely uncharted territory of online video, the studios are reinventing the business model. Their plans are full of possibilities and uncertainties. All assumptions about how entertainment is delivered, how the Internet works and how money can be made are up for grabs.

But as Disney and News Corp. prepare to introduce Movies.com and Sony, Metro-Goldwyn-Mayer, Paramount Pictures, Universal Studios and Warner Bros. unveil Movielink, the question remains: Will these paid online-movie ventures be attractive enough to entice users to migrate from the free, under-the-table services?

There had been attempts in the past to create synergies between different Sony business units, albeit not entirely successful. One of the first synergies Sony Pictures Entertainment found was with Sony Music Entertainment Inc. Michael Schulhof, when he was chief executive of Sony Corporation of America, tried to bring these two business units closer, sometimes at the cost of making enemies. To Sony Pictures, he insisted that soundtracks must feature recording artists from Sony Music. To the music business, he demanded that the artists use actual clips from Sony films whenever possible. Although people resented his interference, Schulhof declared that cooperation had to happen. In forcing the issue, he actually came up with a few successes. One example was Will Smith's first big film, *Bad Boys*, a $16-million action-adventure produced by Don Simpson and Jerry Bruckheimer, which was among Columbia's biggest hits in 1995. Schulhof strong-armed Sony Music into using action sequences from the movie in the music video to promote the soundtrack, and the resulting video was a hit in its own right.

But there were also moments when the efforts to synergize on a larger scale failed to deliver on their promise. One example was a many-spoked deal with Michael Jackson. The joint venture would include six new Jackson albums, Jackson's own Nation Records label, motion pictures, television and short films, and was projected to generate $1 billion in revenue. Jon Peters had originally wooed Jackson into signing, but two months later, Peters departed, and the superstar would only deal with Schulhof in person. Very quickly, the staff at Sony Music began to refer mockingly to Schulhof as "Michael's project manager". During the summer of 1991, a new Jackson album, *Dangerous*, was released on Sony's Epic label and, by previous Jackson standards, was only a modest success with worldwide sales of nine million copies. Jackson's private record label, MJJ Music, found a home at Sony; and one short film was produced, based on *Dangerous*, and ran briefly in theaters. The first full-length feature film for Columbia Pictures, "a musical action-adventure based on an original Jackson idea", was abandoned midway through a development process that involved a dozen rewrites and cost several million dollars.

Even so, marrying hardware with software, music with movies, is more intuitive than creating cross-industry synergies. In many ways, and as proven by the example of Will Smith and the *Bad Boys* movie, it made perfect sense to use Sony's artists to sing Sony movie soundtracks. But when it crossed industry lines, synergy became trickier and less likely to succeed.

Sony Ericsson's *Spider-Man* promo was probably the first successful example for Sony's attempts at the hardware-software combination, although how much the Spiderman character helped the sales of Sony-Ericsson phones is unclear. An early experiment involving Spielberg's film *Hook* was less so. The movie was originally scheduled for release in time for Christmas 1991. Schulhof's idea was to create a series of promotions and premiums designed to augment the film's appeal and ultimate profitability. At Sony Electronic Publishing, engineers developed a video game, which would be ready in advance of the film's release; and the electronics company would provide Walkman models to be awarded to theater audiences in lotteries. For the first time, Schulhof declared expansively, the release of a Hollywood film was being designed to deliver a whole range of synergistic possibilities. In the end, Spielberg was worried that all the commercialism tied to the film would compromise the film's chances of recognition as a creative success, and the campaign was scaled back.

> **"Consistency is what every company strives for. Now it's their job to build off their record." — Joe Roth, Revolution Studios**

Now, Sony has formed a marketing strategy council comprising marketing executives from all over the Sony group. The council meets three or four times a year to discuss ways they could collaborate in marketing strategies precisely in the fashion of *Spider-Man* and Sony Ericsson. The council is still a new concept, and it will be a while before we can judge how well these synergies between the different Sony units will pan out in the long term.

Already, though, Sony Electronics' Clié and VAIO divisions have linked with Sony Pictures Entertainment to allow consumers with those Sony devices to be able to exclusively download the latest Sony movie trailers. With Clié, the mobile handheld organizer, this means consumers can learn about Sony movies anywhere they are. If a Clié user downloads a movie trailer, sees it and likes it, maybe he will tell his friends and word will spread. "Consistency is what every company strives for," says Joe Roth, whose Revolution Studios is producing *XXX* with Sony, and who has been approached to replace Calley when he retires. "Now it's their job to build off their record."

SONY'S RECIPES FOR SUCCESS

- *Understand your businesses*: For any corporation, it is exciting to enter new business realms, take on new challenges, especially ones that you believe can complement and strengthen your existing businesses. But first you have to do your homework and analyze clearly how your new business will benefit your current situation and how your new business will fit into the rest of the company.

- *Hire smartly*: In expanding into new businesses, you may just want to hire the best in that market to help you succeed. When hiring, you have to also be mindful of how well the new managers work with the rest of your existing team. Hiring a good team player is as important as hiring someone with the right expertise.

- *Don't give up easily*: It's not easy to start a new business, so be patient. Don't give up easily when you hit a bump along the way. Evaluate the situation. Identify the obstacles and find ways to overcome them.

- *When in doubt, reuse your success formula*: Sometimes reinventing the wheel, trying new strategies, can help reboot a business that is in trouble. But when you do find a successful formula, why not stick to it? Learn from your successes; reuse and tweak what has worked for you in the past to suit what you are doing now.

- *Share resources and find common ground*: Bringing business units together across industries doesn't have to feel trying. There are often overlaps in strategy and resources. Find the common ground between business units, and where resources overlap. These are the simplest ways of achieving synergy.

NOTES

1.   Lee Smith and Darienne L. Dennis, "Sony Battles Back", *Fortune*, April 15, 1985, p.26.

2.   Phillip McCarthy, "Film Studio Execs Seek The Grail of Synergy", *Sydney Morning Herald*, June 24, 1989, p.41.

3.   William K. Knoedelseder Jr., "CBS Confirms Talks With Sony Over Records Unit", *Los Angeles Times*, October 28, 1987.

4.   *Genryu*, Sony Corporation of America, 1996.

5.   Nancy Griffin and Kim Masters, *Hit and Run: How Jon Peters and Peter Guber Took Sony for a Ride in Hollywood*, Touchstone Books, 1996. Much of the story about Sony's acquisition of Columbia Pictures is drawn from the narrative of this book. It remains the most detailed and candid telling of the acquisition.

6.   Nancy J. Perry, "Will Sony Make it in Hollywood?", *Fortune*, September 9, 1991, p.158.

7.   www.sonypictures.com

8.   V. Dion Haynes, "VOD Pits Studios Against Consumers. Entertainment Industry Tackles Digital Rights", *Chicago Tribune*, February 11, 2002.

Seven

MARKETING 101: BRAND IT!

Founder Akio Morita wanted consumers to pick up a Sony
product and always exclaim, "Ah, It's a Sony!" That distinct
recognition of a Sony product over another brand has
become a Sony trademark, and is one of the reasons it
has the global reach it enjoys. How has it been able to do
this? Not just by being a technological innovator.
This chapter is about how Sony's creative marketers built
a brand for the electronics company that strives always to
spark the imagination of consumers around the world.

When Sony created its artificially intelligent robotic pet in 1999, just finding the right name for the robot took the company three months. Sony's development team and outside brand consultants labored for two months just discussing the idea of what this robotic pet should represent. Was it just a machine? A pseudo pet? A toy? What role would it play in the consumer's life? Once the group decided that the robot should be marketed as a companion for humans, the brand consultants came up with a list of 60 possible names that tied in the idea of companionship. Among the most popular names were AIBO and BOTNIK. After a few weeks of debate, the team eventually settled on AIBO, which in Japanese means "partnership". The first two letters of the name also captured the idea of the robotic pet's "artificial intelligence", with the latter two being adopted from the word "robot". Another month would go by, though, before AIBO the robotic pet would appear in the marketplace. Once a product name is decided, Sony does a legal search to make sure that the name is not being used anywhere else in the world. After all, if it's not the only one, it's not a Sony product.

The care with which Sony named its robotic pet is a clear example of how the company builds and guards its brand. The same drive to be uniquely innovative applies to Sony's marketing strategies as well, resulting in the creation of other quirky made-up product names such as the Tape-corder and the Walkman. Sony's product naming is just as deliberate as its drive to innovate and be a pioneer in technology and, in many ways, was born of necessity.

When Sony first started in the late 1940s, it was a fledgling no-name company trying to take on established family conglomerates such as Matsushita, Toshiba, and the like. As a new company, Sony had to carve out its own niche in the Japanese market. After the end of the Second World War, the old established firms were coming back into the manufacturing business with well-established, familiar brand names. In a society where brand consciousness and brand loyalty are very high, Sony faced a formidable challenge to convince consumers to abandon their favorite brands and buy products from a company with so few employees.

To build the brand, Akio Morita and Masaru Ibuka believed that the company had to get as close to consumers as possible, whether in Japan or abroad. Morita realized early on that although Sony faced considerable challenges of building a brand at home, it was on an equal footing with the Japanese conglomerates when it came to selling to the rest of the world. Top-quality Japanese goods were virtually unknown before the war. The image of anything marked "Made in Japan" had been very low. The overseas market, Morita believed, would be where Sony could carve out a niche and build a renowned brand that could then be leveraged in the Japanese home market. Just as Sony believed as part of its globalization strategy that the corporation should set up manufacturing plants and offices wherever they sold Sony products, the same principles applied to marketing — the actual selling of the products. Showing consumers who you are and what you have was the key to establishing the brand name. When Morita spoke about sales as a form of communication, he meant it in every way possible.

SELLING TO THE WORLD

"Sales is a form of communication. To persuade consumers that Sony
products improve their lives, we must have our own sales channels."

Akio Morita, founder

In the traditional Japanese system for distributing consumer
products, the manufacturers were kept at arm's length from
the consumer. Communication was all but impossible.
There were primary, secondary and, even, tertiary wholesalers
dealing with some goods before they reached a retailer;
layer after layer of middlemen between the maker and the
ultimate user of the product. In a way, this distribution system
served a social purpose in Japan — it provided plenty of jobs
— but it was also costly and inefficient.

With each layer, the price went up, even though some of the
middlemen might not actually come in contact with the
products. Sony realized early on that it could not adopt this
system. Morita believed that the Sony brand was sacred and
that any third or fourth parties handling Sony products simply
wouldn't have the necessary appreciation for the long hours of
research and design that went into each product's
development. To truly protect its brand reputation, Sony had
to have a direct link to its customers, so that it could better
educate them on how to use the products. That meant that
the company had to set up its own outlets and establish its own
sales and distribution system for getting the goods into the
marketplace. In some consumer markets where Sony had little
choice but to adopt some form of a third-party distribution
system, it dealt with dealers, but never through more than one
middleman. At least that way it could get to know the dealers
personally, and help them understand the value of Sony's
products and the uses to which they could be put.

Most important, having control over sales and distribution enabled the company to be more directly involved in protecting the brand name.

Still, it wasn't easy to establish an independent distribution system, especially in the U.S. market where, typically, manufacturers paired with distributors to sell the products to retailers. Sony understood this; so when Morita first planned to market the transistor radio to Americans in 1955, he went to New York to find a dealer who shared Sony's high regard for branding. Much to his surprise, most of the dealers were unimpressed with the precise smallness of the radio that made it an extraordinary invention. In America, the dealers said, everyone wants big radios. "We have big houses, plenty of room. Who needs these tiny things?" But Morita responded: "Yes, the houses are big — even big enough for every family member to have his or her own room where he or she could turn on this tiny radio and listen to whatever pleases him or her without disturbing or bothering anybody else."[1]

Many retailers began to see the logic in Morita's argument, but they also worried that an unknown company like Sony would not attract the necessary wave of interested consumers to ensure the product's success. One of the companies particularly interested in distributing the transistor radio for Sony was Bulova Corp., an established distributor of watches and clocks. Bulova's purchasing officer was impressed with the radio's size and its sophistication and immediately offered to order 100,000 units. At the time, that was an incredible order for Sony, worth several times the electronics company's total capital.

But there would be one condition: the radios would carry the Bulova name, not the Sony name.

The proposal stunned Morita. He and Ibuka had been determined not to be a subcontracted manufacturer for other companies. They wanted to make a name for their company based on the strengths of their own products. The Bulova purchasing officer didn't understand why Sony wouldn't jump at the proposal, as this would surely give it the money it needed for future research and development projects. "Our company name is a famous brand name that has taken over 50 years to establish," the Bulova executive said to Morita. "Nobody has ever heard of your brand name. Why not take advantage of ours?"

Morita understood the Bulova logic, but he replied: "Fifty years ago, your brand name must have been just as unknown as our name is today. I am here with a new product, and I am now taking the first step for the next 50 years of my company. Fifty years from now, I promise you that our name will be just as famous as your company name is today."

Today, more than 50 years later, Bulova remains a watchmaker; it reported net revenues of $10 million in 2001. Sony, on the other hand, reported net revenues of more than $50 billion and is a reputed, globe-straddling consumer-electronics maker of Walkmans, televisions, computers and video games among other things. As it turns out, Morita was right.

SHOW, DON'T TELL

In line with Morita's philosophy that Sony should get as close to consumers as possible, in 1960, he opened a showroom in the Ginza district of Tokyo, which still exists today. The decision he made was an unusual one. As discussed earlier, consumer-electronics companies typically used a network of third-party dealers and retailers to market their products. They didn't have the benefit of owning their own sales force, designing their own displays and controlling how their brand image might be projected. All of that was left in the hands of the dealers. But Sony believed not just in building a good company with solid technological know-how and product line, but also in building a brand. To do so, it needed to take the sales and marketing side of business into its own hands. At the eight-story building in the heart of Tokyo's most prized shopping district, potential customers could handle and try out Sony products with no aggressive salesman around to try to sell them anything, and it quickly became a popular place to visit. For Sony, the showroom's advertising value was enormous. Because Sony was still so new, this was a way to introduce the company to the Japanese consumers, just as later Sony would introduce itself to Americans and Europeans.

To have a showroom in New York quickly became a goal for Sony in the early 1960s. Most people in the U.S. and Europe associated Japan with paper umbrellas, kimonos, toys and cheap trinkets. Morita believed Sony had to reach out to the overseas consumers on their home turf to show them that Sony was more than just cheap imitations. (Morita admitted in his 1985 memoir that, in its early days, Sony, would print the line "Made in Japan" as small as possible, to minimize the stigma that was attached to Japanese products at the time. Once, the company printed it so small on one product that the U.S. Customs asked Sony to make it bigger.)

To dispel the stereotype about Japanese goods, Morita went to New York and surveyed the city, looking for a storefront to show off Sony products. He quickly realized that if the people he wanted to reach were the people who had money and could afford to buy Sony's rather high-priced products, there was only one place to be: Fifth Avenue. He walked up and down Fifth Avenue in mid Manhattan looking at the people and the shops. It was very impressive to him: Tiffany, Cartier, Sak's Fifth Avenue, Bergdorf-Goodman. Morita narrowed his search to the east side of Fifth Avenue between about Forty-fifth and Fifty-sixth because it then seemed the most elegant part of the street.

Morita later wrote that, while he was searching for a suitable ground-floor spot to rent, he noticed that the flags of many nations were on display along the streets but, much to his dismay, there was no Japanese flag. So Morita decided that when Sony opened its showroom, it would be the first to fly the Japanese flag on Fifth Avenue. Today, Sony's original New York and Tokyo showrooms still stand. In Europe, Sony has a showroom in the basement of the Emporio Armani flagship store in Milan, Italy, as well as one in Paris on the Champs d'Elysees.

CREATING A BRAND IDENTITY

We saw earlier the lengths to which Morita and Ibuka went to come up with the perfect name for their corporation. Just as Sony pays meticulous attention to innovating, it also believes in building a strong corporate identity, and tying its products to this brand so that people can recognize and immediately exclaim, "It's a Sony!" Just designing the way the name "Sony" looks on a product is art in itself. The first logotype for the four-letter name made its debut in 1955 on the company's first radio. In those days, the Sony name was displayed in an attenuated, italicized, sans serif typeface set within a vertical rectangle, a very 1950s look. Three years later, when the company finally decided to formally change the name from Tokyo Tsushin Kogyo to Sony, the Sony brand logo changed as well to a horizontally scaled, bold, serif typeface, with copious letter spacing to allow the word to read well on a small product or from a distance. Since then, the logo has evolved through six incarnations, sometimes bearing thinner, bolder or shorter fonts. The current expression has lasted more than 20 years, an eternity in today's corporate environment.

THE S-MARK

According to legend, in 1967, Morita was visiting an electronics show with a group of dignitaries. Scanning the various products, his eyes fixed on a particularly beautiful television, causing him to gesture to his guests: "This is a Sony design. See how fine it is?" Yet on closer inspection, the TV turned out to be a Toshiba product. Embarrassed by the incident, Morita quickly ordered Sony's Corporate Identity Group to design a graphical symbol that could be fixed to all Sony products, making them easy to identify. Thus began the S-mark.

Designed by Sony's logo god, Masaaki Omura, the symbol is composed of seven rows of ascending dots that line up vertically on the left and form a "S" on the right. Used to differentiate Sony's products from look-alike competitors, the S-mark has strengthened and enhanced familiarity of Sony's image in electronics. With the logo-type, the S-mark is the central element in Sony's Visual Identity System, often used with the slogan "It's a Sony" on product packaging, advertising, promotional materials and countless decals, and is stuck onto the products themselves.

Unlike the Sony logo, the S-mark can be removed once the user takes the product home. Used successfully for more than 30 years, the S-mark suddenly disappeared during the summer of 1998, in response to a terse memorandum issued from the Corporate Identity Group. When the Design Center asked for an explanation, they were met with silence.[2]

Whether being used as a housemark, a trademark, a trade name, a company name, or as an endorsement brand, the Sony logo is always shown clearly and conspicuously in the design of a product, packaging scheme, letterhead or building. Within Sony, there are strict rules on how the company would use the Sony name, both internally and on advertising and packaging. For example, the logo should always exist in an "isolation zone" — surrounded by ample blank space in order to display the logo as an independent element. Corporate colors are strictly enforced. There are specific Sony colors by names such as Sony Blue 90, Sony Light Gray 90 and Sony Dark Gray 90, which are to be used on specific products, stationery, packaging, vehicles or buildings. To enforce these guidelines, Sony's Brand Management Office oversees logo usage on a company-wide basis, while individual designers make logo decisions on individual products. Occasionally, of course, mistakes occur. For example, one three-story-high billboard that loomed over New York's Times Square for more than a decade apparently had the four-letter logo placed vertically, an obvious mistake.

In the past, the Sony logo predominated on product packaging and appearance. The marketing of Sony's first products focused almost entirely on building market recognition for the Sony brand. The naming of the products themselves was less of a concern. The first Tape-corder was called the G-Type. The first marketed transistor radio was the TR-55. In recent years, however, with the establishment of the Sony brand, there has been a shift to focus on the more specific sub-brand name such as the Walkman, Discman, Pressman, Trinitron, VAIO, among others. These sub-brand logos no longer just sit there waiting for eyeballs to come to them. They are now designed to explode off the surface, and graphically collide with the surrounding surface in a way that captures the consumers' attention. Their aggressiveness is matched only by their precise placement on the product and by the individuality that Sony designers give to each brand. For example, a design for the Walkman gave feet to each of the letters in the name, signifying the essence of the product's portability. Now, there are more than 400 logos in the current Sony product inventory, running the gamut from simple condensed typefaces to wacky, colorful, hand-drawn scripts that take product imagery to a whole new level.

THE PLAYSTATION NAME

First impressions are often the best when designing something new. Since Sony had no experience in the video-game market, creating a suitable logo and product name was difficult. Dozens of names were proposed and rejected before a Sony marketing executive suggested the word "PlayStation". Even though rival Yamaha had already trademarked the name, then-president Nobuyuki Idei liked it so much that he agreed to acquire it for an undisclosed sum rather than search for an alternative.

Once the name was established, the task of developing the logo was given to graphic designer Manabu Sakamoto, who, in a flurry of activity, created more than 50 graphic variations on the letters P and S during a two-week period in October/November 1993.

"I tried every imaginable permutation," the designer recalled in Paul Kunkel's book about Sony's Design Centers, *Digital Dreams*. "Eventually, I stood the letter P on end and treated the S like a shadow." Thrilled by the result, Sakamoto drew three variations, which received approval from Idei. For consistency, the P would always appear in red and the S would always appear in three colors.

COMPOSING A MARKETING CAMPAIGN

With a definite logo and brand identity comes a definite marketing strategy. Not surprisingly, like everything else Sony does, the marketing campaign itself is a careful artistic design, an interactive journey consumers have to experience.

Take the Walkman campaign, for example. Everything, from the name to the way Sony tried to generate interest and excitement over the Walkman, was entirely in tune with Sony style. Morita orchestrated every aspect of the Walkman campaign, beginning with the press conference to introduce the product. Normally, product introductions are held indoors. But when journalists arrived at the Sony building in the Ginza on June 22, 1979, they were escorted onto buses and taken to Yoyogi Park, where each was handed a Walkman and asked to push the play button. While they stood under the trees listening to a recorded pitch with background music in stereo, Sony staffers and models demonstrated how to enjoy the Walkman on roller skates, skateboards, or riding a tandem bicycle on a date. The idea was to tie the Walkman to youth culture, to a cool look. And who better to convince first than the journalists who write about and critique the product?[3]

"I tried every imaginable permutation. Eventually, I stood the letter P on end and treated the S like a shadow."
— Manabu Sakamoto, Sony designer

Morita also had a hand in the early print ads, which were aimed at the young and active and emphasized speed and mobility: a girl with long blond hair bent low on her racing bike; a blond roller-skater in summer shorts; a roller-skating couple, hand in hand. The Sony Walkman was positioned as a passkey to youth and sportiness. One poster placed a Walkman alongside three pairs of shoes. The banner read: "Why man learned to walk."

Less overtly, the early campaigns emphasized the lightness of the headphones and the stylishness of the earpieces compared to the bulky, earmuff look of conventional earphones. In the first poster for the Tokyo launch, a tall, leggy American girl in leotard and heels grooves to the music coursing through her Walkman headphones, her left arm thrown exuberantly upward. Just behind her stands an elderly Japanese Buddhist monk in summer kimono. On his shaved head, he wears clunky old-fashioned phones, and observes the young lady with a look of admiration and envy. Other ads featured two comely models in evening dress and headphones on the deck of a ship in New York Harbor, or a blond Cleopatra in a sheer bathing costume reclining at the edge of a swimming pool at dusk. In every case, the images reinforced the notion that the Walkman and its stylish headphones were a fashion statement.

The emphasis on fashion and youth was partly Morita's response to uneasiness inside Sony about a product that required headphones. But Morita had already anticipated this objection and was ready with an answer: Sony would create a new fashion, a "headphone culture".

On July 17, 1979, the Walkman was officially launched in Japan, more than three weeks behind Morita's deadline. For a month, nothing happened. Then, from mid August on, dealers had trouble keeping their shelves stocked. The first 30,000 units were gone by the middle of September and, for the rest of the year, production capacity had to be doubled and tripled every month. The first buyers were music fans in their mid twenties, but by the fall, the average age of customers fell further, and the Walkman had become the fashionable new way for teenagers to listen to music.

Foreign sales of the Walkman weren't due to begin until February 1980, but advertising had already been placed in the fall. Aware that "Walkman" was Japanese English, Morita had approved a suggestion from the advertising department that the product be sold under different names in different countries. The player was to be called "Sound-About" in the U.S. and "Stowaway" in Britain, where "Sound-About" was already registered. In Sweden, where the lawlessness conveyed by "Stowaway" was deemed objectionable, it was named "Freestyle".

However, in November 1979, Morita telephoned Sony from Paris and said he had decided that the product should be sold as Walkman everywhere. All summer and fall, tourists and airline flight crews had been bringing the player home from Japan, and a Walkman had been given as a gift to musicians in the Berlin and New York Philharmonic orchestras. Morita found himself besieged by friends in New York, London and Paris asking how they could lay hands on a Walkman for their children.

Morita also realized very quickly that the name "Walkman" had global appeal regardless of whether or not it was proper English. When Kozo Ohsone, general manager of the Tape Recorder division, pointed out that advertising using other names had begun, Morita replied that his next call would be to Marketing at Park Ridge, New Jersey, and hung up.

ORIGINS OF THE NAME "WALKMAN"

When the name "Walkman" was first proposed for Sony's first portable stereo device, it wasn't a popular choice. This was partly because of a concern among Sony executives that the word was grammatically incorrect in English, and therefore would confuse Western consumers. At the time, Morita's one major request for the naming of the device was this: it had to project the fun and dynamic image that would be the marketing campaign for this product. Most buyers, Morita presumed, would be young people; so he wanted the young staff members to come up with a name that was in tune with their own generation. At the time, the super-hero icon Superman was popular. The name "Walkman", had a similar logical origin and ring as "Superman". It was also, in a sense, a spin-off of a previous product, the Pressman, a small monaural tape recorder launched in 1977. And ultimately, the fact that consumers would be able to listen to music on the product while out walking on the streets made the name "Walkman" quite appropriate.

Between 1979 and 1990, Sony developed and launched more than 80 different models of the increasingly portable stereo player. In the process, Walkman became a household word around the world and, as Morita had predicted, established headphone music on the move as a singular feature of international youth culture. The phenomenon has always been closely associated with Morita personally. When he was knighted at the British embassy in Tokyo in October 1992, two English tabloids headlined the story, "Arise, Sir Sony Walkman".[4]

Ohga, by his own admission, never paid any attention to the Walkman. Reflecting on his attitude as cumulative sales approached 350 million units at the end of 1998, he reaffirmed his admiration for Morita's market sense: "I could never be bothered because it had no technical interest. When they showed it to me, I was preoccupied with CDs and optical laser technology. Frankly I couldn't see why Sony should make a product that was boring technically. And that is the major difference between me and Mr. Morita. He had the merchant's intuition that allowed him to see what it would become. If it had been up to me, it would never have happened."

WALKMAN LAWSUIT

In June 2002, the Supreme Court of Austria ruled that Sony Corp. had lost the trademark right on its Walkman brand, now commonly used as a generic name for portable cassette players of any brand. Although this ruling applies only to Austria, where a distributor of electronics goods used the word Walkman to describe all portable cassette players it sells, Sony Corp. contends that it hurts the corporation's brand image.

The ruling originated from a lawsuit filed against the Austrian distributor in 1994, in which Sony had contended that the term "Walkman" should only apply to portable cassette players made by Sony because the brand is registered as its trademark all over the world. The ruling by the Austrian Supreme Court stated that Sony had not taken steps to prevent the widespread use of Walkman as a common noun. The word could be found in a German dictionary, where it was defined as "a portable cassette tape player". Some legal experts in Austria are now concerned that other European courts may adopt the Austrian ruling since Austrian trademark rights are based on criteria set by the European Union.

At the time of the ruling, Sony executives expressed regret over the court's decision, saying that the lesson learnt was that "Sony must be an activist about protecting its trademarks and brands... It must take action against others who abuse our brand or else we give them an excuse to ruin our brand image."

Now, Sony has a "Walkman" committee that regularly monitors the usage of the brand name. The Brand Management office within Sony has also sent out a memo to all Sony subsidiaries worldwide to ask them to be diligent about protecting the Walkman name.

Among Sony's products, the Walkman brand is probably the most popularly and frequently used name. Should other products run into the same type of trademark controversies, Sony will also establish monitoring committees to ensure no one abuses the Sony sub-brands, Sony executives say.

Perhaps that was the genius of Morita, who was the most avid promoter of Sony. Whereas his co-founder and mentor Ibuka's strengths were in searching for new technologies, Morita had a sharp eye for making possible the seemingly impossible and the Walkman provides clear evidence of his ingenious marketing skills.

OOZE CONFIDENCE

Just as innovation has been at the heart of the Sony corporate culture and spirit from the outset, so too has been the drive to build a global brand. Perhaps the fact that Sony was a no-name company amidst giant Japanese conglomerates sparked Morita's ambitious drive to make the Sony name recognized and respected in the international consumer-electronics market.

Morita believed confidently that the Sony name would have global reach, and it would be well known in every household. Living in New York (he moved his family there in 1963) enabled Morita to wade into the launch with his full power as a salesman. At home, he spent his nights in front of the television, studying commercials, and was amused and impressed by Volkswagen's humorous campaign organized around the notion of a lemon. This was around the time when Sony was trying to enter the U.S. market with its micro-televisions. Through connections, Morita was able to arrange a lunch meeting with William Bernbach, creative director of Doyle Dane Bernback, VW's advertising agency in America. Morita and Bernbach hit it off at once. The Sony showroom was near Bernbach's office and he had long admired the Sony products on display there. But when Morita told him that Sony's budget would be $500,000 a year to start, Bernbach replied that the agency minimum was $1 million. Morita assured him that the Sony name would shortly be bigger than Volkswagen and persuaded him to accept the account.

Bernbach was convinced and his team created a series of successful print ads all to emphasize the lightweight portability of Sony's televisions. One illustrated the benefits of "Tummy Television", showing a portly gentleman in bed at night enjoying a lightweight five-inch Sony propped on his belly. Another, "Telefishin", featured a nine-inch Sony TV in a rowboat on the lake, and another highlighted the ambulatory four-inch "Walkie-Watchie". The light humor of the ads generated a fair bit of consumer attention. When reporters phoned to request a visit from someone to explain the product, they were treated to a sales pitch from Morita himself and, perhaps inspired by his showmanship even in English, stories appeared in *Time*, *Newsweek* and *Fortune*. The micro-TVs began to sell. Despite a price of $250 at a time when a 27-inch set sold for $150, sales climbed steeply. By 1969, Sony had sold one million units.

The Bernbach advertisements, as well as Morita's Walkman campaign, are good examples of how Sony concocts marketing campaigns out of the ordinary, inviting consumers to put aside what they know as reality and dream a bit. Sony would go on to create many memorable advertisements and marketing campaigns — all of which are based on a fundamental principle of inspiring the consumer, challenging what they know as reality and possibility. Perhaps, though, the whole thrust and essence of Sony's marketing logic is captured in the single phrase: "Do you dream in Sony?"

SONY'S RECIPES FOR SUCCESS

- *Brand values carry you far*: Recognizing that brand values matter sounds obvious, but it is the first step to creating a reputation for your brand. You want to create a reputation such that consumers see your brand or a product carrying your brand name and immediately think: trustworthy, solid. You want a brand that makes people want to buy your products.

- *Show. Don't tell*: Advertising on television and in the print media (and now on the Internet) are traditional ways of marketing your brand. But sometimes you have to show, not tell. Build a showroom on a busy commercial corner in a major city. Show off your products. Let consumers come into your store and play with the gadgets or services so that they can experience first-hand the possibilities your product or service offers them.

- *Pay attention to detail*: It's all in the detail. From how you select your name to how you present your company's image, if you pay attention to the little details, it will help you establish deeper brand value. For example, when you name your products, think of names that are easy to remember, punchy and have a ring to them. You want consumers to immediately associate your product with your company.

- *Be confident*: Nothing adds more value to your brand than confidence. It can show through the way you compose your advertising campaigns, the way you deal with distributors and retailers. Your confidence gives your retailers confidence to sell your products well as opposed to your competitors' products.

NOTES

1.   Morita et al, op. cit.

2.   Paul Kunkel, *Digital Dreams: The Work of the Sony Design Center*, Universe, 1999.

3.   *Genryu*, Sony Corporation of America, 1996.

4.   Nathan, op. cit.

Eight

PAY ATTENTION: IT'S ALL IN THE DETAILS

Sony used to bank on its technological innovations
(such as the compact disc) for success in bringing in
licensing fees in addition to product sales. But as
technologies became more standardized and accessible to
others, Sony started losing its edge. So it started to
differentiate its products by pushing out new shapes,
colors, sizes and combinations of features before its
competitors. This chapter explores how Sony's obsession
with detail is paying off.

I n the past, being first to market and being the most innovative, with high-quality, low-cost production were enough to ensure success. But today, products must entertain on every level and have a spirit and personality that has to be conveyed through design. Design has become as important in the preservation of a brand's image as the product's technological excellence and capabilities. Sony's success in promoting a solid brand image is a testament to its keen understanding that design quality and consistency — from the color of the shell to the naming of the product — are a top priority. It is from this dedication and careful planning that Sony's image has remained intact, earning great awareness and respect over the years.

With technology now within everyone's grasp, and prices dropping every year, consumer electronics would become commodity items, indistinguishable from one another, if people did not yearn for products with an image, tactile quality, symbolism and story that give the products value and meaning. As Norio Ohga said when he was chairman of Sony in the early 1990s, "The product itself must be good, but it must also make the customer think, 'I'm glad I bought it; I'm glad I use it; I'm glad I have it.'"

Great products and the experience they deliver to consumers play an important, even crucial, role in a world in which mediocrity is the norm. But as technologies change, markets divide into new niches and consumer tastes evolve in ways that few can predict. In the past, Sony typically had ownership of

"The product itself must be good, but it must also make the customer think, 'I'm glad I bought it; I'm glad I use it; I'm glad I have it.'"
— Norio Ohga, Sony chairman (1995–1999)

a new product market for at least a year, sometimes two years, before rivals were able to catch up. Now, that market lead no longer exists. The standardization of technology and the fact that the competitor pool has expanded beyond the confines of consumer electronics have made it difficult for Sony always to stay ahead, even for a few months. Along with this rapid regeneration of technology and products, the consumers' tastes have also become more fickle. The abundance of new gadgetry in the marketplace has made them want the best, the newest, and they often abandon past loyalties they might have had to brands.

The comfort of the past and the knowable present have given way to a brave new world populated by a new breed of individuals raised on the Internet, having no loyalty to the analog technology of the past, to the Sony name or anything else. For these new consumers, the old rules that governed society no longer apply. Every rule written in the analog age must be re-examined, and some turned inside out, to accommodate the digital age that is now upon us.

From a technological point of view, Sony has always striven to live up to consumers' expectations. Whether in the way Sony brands its products, or the way it designs the look, feel and symbolism of its products, its engineers, designers and marketers pore over every little detail, piecing together what will ultimately come to represent the brand that everyone now knows.

ATTENTION! DETAILS!

Even in the analog era, Sony had a keen understanding that appearances mattered. Masaru Ibuka once said that innovation comes from the heart. In keeping with this motto, the aim of every Sony product was to delight the consumers and stretch their individual and collective imaginations, and that meant building high-performance products that had beauty and a distinctive flair, that were both easy to use and fun to operate. It was no surprise, therefore, that Sony established its own design center early on in its evolution.

In 1961, long before graphic or industrial design became mainstream in Japan, Sony founded its Design Center in Atsugi, Tokyo. The Design Center aggressively pursued a product design and packaging program within the company to create products that consumers would look at and exclaim, "Ah, it's a Sony!"

Since the first Design Center opened in Tokyo, Sony has established a dozen more studios around the world spanning North America, South America, Europe and Asia. Like their counterparts in research and development, designers work with one another across geographical boundaries to coordinate designs for product launches. The sole job of the designers and engineers who make up Sony's Design Center is to think about how people will choose, receive and experience technology and entertainment, and turn that into Sony products. This focus on design has become increasing important at Sony, which used to rely on technological innovation, profits from licensing fees and product sales for its successes. But as technologies became more standardized and accessible to others, Sony started losing its edge. Design then has become a means through which the corporation has been able to differentiate its products. By pushing out new shapes, colors, sizes and combinations of features before its competitors, it has maintained a certain brand image of what a Sony should be like.

The challenge to Sony is greater now than ever. With technology driving society at a speed unparalleled in history, a new consumer is emerging: one suspicious of traditional looks and offerings, unmoved by advertising and contemptuous of mass media. The old view of products as stand-alone devices is beginning to change. Now, products have new relationships with one another, relationships that Sony has identified as connectivity, centered largely around the Internet. Even voice recorders and digital cameras, which may seem unrelated, will share the same form of digital information — speaking the same language and working together in ways that allow each product to become part of a seamless media landscape. Creating the demand for such complex connectivity between gadgets is a daunting challenge but one which Sony must meet if it is to survive in the digital era.

CREATE THE LOOK

The VAIO computer is the embodiment of this new reality of connectivity. It has not only driven Sony's entry into the personal computer market, it has also defined a key part of the company's current consumer-electronics strategy.

When the first VAIO computer was introduced in 1997, it was a latecomer in the personal computer market. PC-clone makers had already turned the product into a low-priced commodity manufactured with razor-thin margins. In the U.S., consumers were beginning to find PCs that cost less than $600 for basic word-processing and perhaps Internet surfing. The typical computer was a white box with a basic hard drive, disk drive, keyboard and monitor. The differences between brands, if there were any at all, were almost indistinguishable. But even so, Sony designers were convinced that the company had to enter the PC market quickly, even if it had to play catch-up initially.

With the Internet changing the landscape of entertainment and communications and many of Sony's own consumer electronics looking more like computers themselves, Sony engineers knew that it would be vital for the company to release a line of desktop and portable computers that would allow them to spearhead the move toward digital convergence. How VAIO came to be one of the most recognizable laptop brands, with its now well-known, sleek, silvery purple cover and curvy brand logo, provides a telling story of how Sony's attention to detail created that brand image attention to.[1]

To make a difference in PC design, Sony engineers decided that the new personal computer needed a unique name and concept, and a design and an interface on the screen that would make it stand out from the typical Windows computer. Because it was a Sony, the computer would have to offer the best video and audio quality. Because it would have to be in sync with Sony video cameras, digital still cameras and other products, the computer's inputs and outputs would have to be state of the art. Combining those two concepts, Sony's designer guru and director of the Design Center, Teiyu Goto, made several suggestions to the New Business Group, including the acronym, VAIO, originally a short form of "video audio input output". (As the product evolved so too did the meaning of the acronym. It currently stands for "video audio integrated operation".) Like the Macintosh, which most consumers knew by the abbreviation "Mac", the VAIO name was short and distinctive and could easily be marketed as a catchy brand name. "But the name alone wasn't enough," Goto said at the time. "It also needed a story or legend that would give the name importance. Like the Walkman, I wanted VAIO to become a name that would last for a hundred years."

Goto conceived of the VAIO not as a new product, but something ancient that had only recently been discovered. He imagined that he was roaming the desert in some distant land, far from civilization. After wandering for days, he encountered a disturbance in the ground, began to dig, uncovered an artifact that bore a faint inscription and traced the letters with his fingers in the sand. V...A...I...O...

Translating this imaginary sand inscription into a logo, Goto drew the V and A as a continuous wavy line followed by a separate I and O. When the Sony marketing manager saw the logo, the story goes, he pointed out that V and A looked like an analog sine wave, while the I and O resembled the numbers one and zero on which computer binary language is based. Once the VAIO logo had been decided on, everyone on the development team — engineers, designers, software writers and marketers — wore the logo on their shirt or jacket to remind them of who they were and what they were doing. VAIO would not be a traditional Sony product. It was supposed to be a little different, and that difference was critical to the success of the project and to Sony's evolution.

Since its launch in 1997, VAIO has evolved from a made-up word into a brand name for Sony's global strategy describing the shift from analog to digital technology. As Sony's product line continues to evolve from many stand-alone analog devices to a family of connected digital appliances, the VAIO computer serves as one of the linchpins, a key connection point.

On a visual level, Sony engineers wanted VAIO to harmonize with the rest of Sony's audio/video family. So form and color were of critical importance in the designing of the VAIO. Black, the designers decided, was too heavy for a home product, so they chose a medium gray. But they also wanted an accent color. The end result was a gray/violet, which gave the product a softer quality that would convey a playfulness and elegance. As the VAIO concept evolved from a brand of personal computer to a global strategy for digital convergence, the color known as "Goto purple" (after the designer) signifies VAIO connectivity the same way that bright yellow identifies the Sports Walkman.

PACKAGE WELL

Sony's attention to detail isn't confined to the look of the product. It goes as far as the look of the box in which the product comes. Packaging, after all, is what first draws a consumer to a product. In many countries, packaging is treated as a form of marketing — something the consumer will throw away. But in Japan, product presentation is considered an art form, layered with symbolism and meaning injected into even the simplest product container. Walk into any grocery store in Japan, and you will be astonished by the attention to detail and presentation: even fish is laid out onto shaved ice in a precise pattern; every piece of fruit is scrupulously cleaned and positioned for maximum visual appeal; and the packaged goods are extraordinarily detailed and always contain some form of humor, emotion or surprise. Sometimes the packages tell a story centered around a character that might be printed on a cookie, or feature a treasure hunt that will entertain consumers while they eat the snack.[2]

> In Japan, product presentation is considered an art form, layered with symbolism and meaning injected into even the simplest product container.

Humor, friendliness, honesty, lively color and inventive shapes are all part of the Sony approach. Depending on the time, the product and the intended audience, the package may be slick and bright, with lavish use of heavy-metal inks and elaborate coatings, or it may be plain or understated, using eco-friendly materials. The one constant in Sony's packaging design is change. No single style can represent the breadth of what Sony has to offer, one packaging designer at Sony said. Graphic designing and packaging are viewed as clothing, which you can change every day. But changing a particular packaging doesn't mean you change the image.

For Walkmans and VAIOs, the packaging is straightforward. Consumers already know the brand well. When they arrive at a store to buy a portable stereo, they might have decided already that they want a Sony Walkman. So the pressure is less on the packaging of the Walkman boxes and more on the quality of the technology and the shape and size of the

Walkman product. Tape cassette and MiniDisc media packaging, on the other hand, pose a challenge when it comes to marketing. Since all blank media are similar in the customer's mind, the key issues are brand identity, product description and a recognizable color. What will make a consumer pick up your blank tape and not some other brand's? Immense efforts have been made to develop the right design and color for the packaging of Sony's media products. With competition increasing in the late 1980s, Sony's Tokyo designers decided to give all video media a unified look. After weeks of research and testing, they decided that the best color for the global market was a bright lemon yellow. Concepts for each tape product were generated. The design process went smoothly until then-president Norio Ohga pointed out that Sony's lemon yellow concepts were too close to the "Kodak yellow" used on film boxes known throughout the world. To avoid consumer confusion, Ohga suggested that Sony adopt a dark, bold red globally.

It was assumed that Sony marketers in the U.S. would adopt the red strategy as well. But U.S. executives wanted to apply a unified color strategy to all consumer media, including computer diskettes and batteries, and market research indicated that Americans preferred blue to red. But Ohga wanted Sony to have a single global color. He envisioned walking into any store in the world and picking out Sony media from its competitors because of its red packaging. But the U.S. marketers demurred. Since Ohga was planning to leave the president's office to become global chairman, he left the decision to his successor Nobuyuki Idei, who accepted the local approach. Fortunately for Sony, the blue strategy has been a success in the U.S.

REINVENT AND REFINE

Sometimes a design doesn't have to be dramatic for it to make its presence known in a crowded market of similar products. Take the Clié, for example, a latecomer to a handheld-organizer market that was already saturated with Palms and pocket personal computers from major computer manufacturers. But with wireless devices becoming an important part of its business strategy, Sony believed it had to enter the handheld market. The question to be answered, though, was how it would distinguish itself.

In typical fashion, Sony approached the design of the product from a different perspective. The handhelds available on the market all generally served the same purpose: they were the electronic version of the business diary, with software to keep phone numbers, addresses and appointments. Typically, users were businesspeople. The Sony Clié is different. Standing for "Communication Linkage for Information and Entertainment", the Clié stresses its entertainment aspects. Equipped with software to download content, the Clié enables users to surf the Internet for their favorite music in MP3 format or movie trailers, and to download and store them. It is equipped with an output for headphones so that the handheld can also double as a portable MP3 music player. One of the most recent models, the NR-70, has an embedded digital camera, which consumers could use to take pictures and send them to friends immediately. It also has a built-in knob that mimics that which Japanese mobile phones have for scrolling the screen. With Japanese users as their first test market, Sony designers put the knob scroll in the NR-70 thinking that it would be a familiar motion for users who are used to scrolling through their mobile phones to surf the

Web. It is precisely this kind of detail that distinguishes the Clié from other handheld devices.

The fundamental data-storing functions haven't changed on the Clié, but the logic of the Sony design put the consumers' convenience and interests first. The most striking evidence of this is the Clié NR-70's built-in mini-keyboard. Because sometimes the graffiti writing (the term used to describe how text is entered into handheld organizers) isn't easily picked up by the handheld operating system, Sony has installed a keyboard into its device so that users can just "type" the data into the gadget without the hassle of trying to write clearly enough for the graffiti software to make out the letters. With all of the care that went into designing the Clié, it is not surprising that the Sony handheld has been able to quickly gain a strong position in the U.S. handheld market, its largest market.

KNOW YOUR TARGET AUDIENCE

Until very recently, no market research, focus groups or user studies were ever conducted at Sony's Design Center to find out what consumers were thinking or what they wanted. Sony has always stood by the belief that it would allow room for creativity rather than simply dish out assignments to designers before they could be permitted to think about design. Seeing themselves, ultimately, as consumers, Sony designers pay close attention to emerging trends and shifts in technology that could influence Sony's next round of products. Putting this information together, designers can often make educated guesses that result in products that remain ahead of the curve and, thus, pull the market in Sony's direction.

After all, one of Sony's fundamental principles of design and innovation is to always lead and never copy. In design, that principle translates into a philosophical belief that market research is not useful because research, by its very nature, is backward-looking. Sony executives say that their biggest product successes have not been due to any systematic effort. They have happened because a particular designer or engineer or product planner had a vision for products such as the Walkman, the Handycam, or PlayStation, rallied others within the company to support that vision and pushed the products through the system. Some of the stories of how these products came about have already been detailed in earlier chapters and provide evidence to back the claims of Sony executives.

These product successes have taught Sony management to support individual initiative within the company. But the process was risky because, until recently, there was no formal mechanism for testing new product ideas. Occasionally, a designer will work on instinct and develop a product such as the Walkman that defines a generation. But sometimes the instinct can also end in failure. By relying on instinct rather than market research or trend analysis, it's hard to know which product ideas have the best chance for success.

To increase the success rate and propel Sony into new lines of business, one Sony Design Center manager has spearheaded a process for identifying societal change and designing products for new types of users by recalling the experience gained from earlier ventures. One of the most successful of these ventures was the line of children's products called My First Sony. In retrospect, it was an obvious idea: redesign the Sony

Walkman, boombox, Watchman, walkie-talkie and radio into products that would appeal to young children as well as their parents. The shapes of the first My First Sonys were inventive, with oversized handles and contrasting colors that had never been seen in a Sony product before. But they missed the mark because not enough children were consulted during the development. The designs reflected an adult view of what a child would want. For the second series, the designers led a team that began not with concepts or color studies, but by imagining how the products would be used by four–to–eight-year-olds in the home. They sketched various scenarios showing a revised My First Sony line in real-world situations, expanding the line by adding an electronic sketchpad that connected to a color TV, and gave the new designs a more vibrant look and feel. Bolder, more saturated colors and geometric elements made the products jump off the shelf, clearly signifying their purpose as toys, but without requiring a complete retooling.

The success of My First Sony was also an important reminder for Sony designers to always think like consumers and understand the different lifestyles they lead. After all, that's the whole point of making products, so that people will use them. With society and technology changing faster than ever, trend research is merely a way of recording data that will soon become history. By the time a company like Sony can identify a trend and react to it by developing a new product, the phenomenon will have already passed, leaving their product behind the curve. Focus groups are equally problematic, because there is no commonly accepted means of testing buyers' preferences. Test subjects will often respond in a false way, hoping to please the test giver by saying that they like, and would probably buy, a product — even if they don't like it at all. Often, focus groups can only tell you about products they use today, reflecting decisions they made in the past. Offering them products that put those decisions in doubt is difficult enough. Asking people to tell you what decisions they will make in the future is even more difficult. For this reason, designers must rely on a certain amount of intuition when crafting a new product.

To overcome these hurdles, Sony has devised an elaborate model for thinking about its target audience. By dividing its audience into five distinct groups, the Design Center can focus products on individuals and niches rather than a "one style fits all" approach, which often results in one style that fits no one very well. For example, one group, which Sony designers call the "Reactors", are people born in the streets, or who wish they were. They used to watch MTV but don't anymore. They are edgy, rebellious, suspicious of power and authority, and have no particular preferences in the conventional sense. Quickly bored by the present, Reactors want technology to be changeable, adaptable, mutable, futuristic and weapon-like. Typically ranging in age from mid teens to mid 20s, Reactors enjoy compact designs that are "retro-futuristic", with textured surfaces and color preferences that include gray/white as well as bright blue, neon yellow, and red. Sony's Street Style headphones, Street Style Discman, and the PlayStation are precisely designed with Reactors in mind.

TARGET GROUPS

- *The Arbiter of Style*: Sometimes referred to as "Urban Connoisseurs" or "Label Junkies", this group respects products that have design integrity and possess a higher level of "taste" than the other groups. Having traveled the world and been exposed to many cultures and lifestyles, they are materialistic collectors of both ideas and things, and are very selective, often purchasing products before the mass audience weighs in.

- *The Virtual Professional*: A pampered, high-maintenance, hard-charging individual, the Virtual Professional may be an executive, entrepreneur or an ambitious salary employee driven by career goals, which means they are often disconnected from "real life", family and friends. Instead, their connection is to technology, which they use to insulate themselves. They are the "early adopters" who buy the first new gadget, have no trouble learning a new graphical interface and love features that make mundane tasks easier and fun.

- *The Homelander*: The polar opposite to the Virtual Professional, the Homelander is domestic, family-loving, practical and a "follower" who takes pride in work. For these people, technology must be family-friendly and "humanized". They prefer the look and function of old technology, which feeds their love of nostalgia. My First Sony, for example, was ideal for Homelanders and their child.

- *Active senior citizens who are "Off Their Rockers"*: The wealthiest of all groups, senior citizens represent a gold mine for product developers. More secure and physically active than ever, this segment wants technology that is easy to learn and use. This group has money to spend for products that widen their world. The key, though, is simplicity. If a Rocker cannot understand something at a glance, he soon loses interest.

Source: Paul Kunkel's *Digital Dreams*

One of Sony's central philosophies has always been this: products and services must be of the highest quality and offer the best value. At a time when every manufacturer has access to the same technology and offers products of uniform quality at every price point, consumers have become so demanding that they will not tolerate a product that doesn't perform well on every level. For designers to succeed in this crowded and competitive environment, they must appeal to consumers' hearts as well as their minds. Also, both the products and the people who design them must be forward-looking. After all, true identity is not just about how the product looks. It's about satisfying the consumer. Even when the consumer isn't using the product, he should feel happy that he owns it.

DREAM IN SONY

Since its inception, the Design Center's most important role has really been to dream, to visualize, to ponder the future and allow the designers' imaginations to take flight. At Sony's Design Centers around the world, the closets, shelves and hard disks are filled with drawings and models that may one day become products. Some represent incremental improvements on existing technology or put a current product to a new and interesting use. Others are more outrageous and may never actually achieve product status.

Either way, Sony encourages its designers to dream. And from these dreams, it has given us computers with built-in digital cameras, and handheld organizers with built-in keyboards, and a whole host of other products. Idei puts it best: "You see things as they are and ask: why? We dream things that never were and ask: why not?"

SONY'S RECIPES FOR SUCCESS

- *Appearances matter*: First impressions are lasting, even in the business world. How do you capture the attention of your consumers? Everything from the color of your product, to the shapes of the knobs and the look of the product as a whole, all contribute to the consumers' first impressions of your product and, in turn, your company.

- *Stretch people's imagination*: Don't just design your product generically, like the next competitor. Make it unique. Weave a story for the product's origins. Stretch people's imagination. Whether it be the position of the knobs or the materials used for the product, be unique and wow people!

- *Present it well*: The packaging matters just as much as the product itself. For many products, consumers don't see the product until they purchase the packaged goods, take it home and open it up. So the packaging becomes the first impression you give consumers.

- *Know your audience*: Design products and services with your target consumers in mind. This helps you shape the way you present your products or services, gives you a better sense of what these consumers might want. This way, you are more likely to end up with a product or service that is more welcomed and more successful.

NOTES

1.   Kunkel, op. cit., the source of many of the anecdotes in this chapter.

2.   Sony corporate website, www.sony.net.

Additional information in this chapter is drawn from interviews with Mina Naito, Masanobu Sakaguchi, Jyunji Tsuyuki and Eiichi Yamamoto, Sony employees in the U.S. and Japan.

Nine

"CO-OPETITION": SLEEPING WITH THE ENEMY

In this increasingly connected world, there's too much information-and-technology development for any one organization to maintain the resources required to handle it all. So partnerships and acquisitions have gone beyond being strategic options; for companies like Sony that are faced with razor-thin profit margins in consumer electronics, partnerships couldn't be more important. This chapter tells how Sony — typically a corporation that likes to go it alone — is learning slowly but surely how to work with others.

I n the relatively well-ordered, predictable business universe that prevailed through most of the 20th century, we were safe in assuming the constancy of certain bitter rivalries: The Coca-Cola Company versus PepsiCo Inc.; General Motors Corp. versus Ford Motor Company. But today, although some of those rivalries may endure, a great many others are subject to dramatic reversal at almost any time. Companies are cross-investing, putting money in what used to be their enemy's pockets, so to speak. They are joining up in collaboration to develop new technologies. They are forming soft alliances in marketing campaigns. They are sharing in licensing agreements, research consortia, supply agreements, and many other configurations — all blurring the boundaries between intra-firm transactions and those that extend beyond its confines. In particular, the convergence of the Internet, the media and entertainment companies has created some strange bedfellows, such as the mega-merger of media giants America Online and Time Warner. But troubled though some couplings may have turned out to be, the new digital era is forcing once-sworn enemies to let down their guard and work together on one level or another. Welcome to the 21st century, and the beginning of a new business era.

The new relationships in this new era are neither just intra-firm synergies nor cooperation at arm's length. Rather, they stand somewhere in between. Globally, the number of cross-border inter-firm agreements jumped from 1,760 in 1990 to nearly 4,600 in 1995. U.S. firms participated in 80 per cent of them, European Union firms in about 40 per cent, and Japanese firms, like Sony, in 38 per cent. Some alliances are no more than fleeting encounters, lasting only as long as it takes one partner to establish a beachhead in a new market. Others are the prelude to a full merger of two or more companies' technologies and capabilities. Whatever the duration and objectives of business alliances, they have drastically changed and complicated the definition of business rivalry. In the past, the relationship was pure and simple — it was you versus me. Today's rivalries, however, are complex and sometimes even confusing. They have been extended and neatly renamed "co-opetition", where firms that may compete in one realm may cooperate in another market space. There are no longer clear lines that divide friends from foes. Groups of firms can come together to compete with another consortium of firms. At the same time, firms that cooperate within an alliance at one level may remain fierce competitors with one another.[1]

For Sony, a company that has taken pride in its reputation as a "do-it-yourself" innovator, the rapid regeneration of old technology and the introduction of new ones have challenged its ability to keep up with all the latest trends. Its competitors have grown in number, extending far beyond the confines of the consumer-electronics sector to include rivals ranging from chip-makers and PC manufacturers to movie studios and record labels. While it has tried to broaden its business internally, adding to its portfolio of companies a mobile-phone joint venture, a movie studio, a record label and a video-game business, it has recognized that it needs to redefine its goals and work with others in aspects of its business. Slowly but surely, Sony — a company that prided itself on generating its own innovations — is slowly beginning to reach out to other corporations. This new business era demands that Sony make an immediate adjustment of its long-held attitude that if it's not invented at Sony, it's not the best. Sony Computer Entertainment, maker of the Sony PlayStation, for example, has a joint venture with Toshiba Corp. and International Business Machines Corp. to make a super processing chip for the PlayStation 3, due to be released in 2005. But, at the same time, Sony's VAIO product group locks horns with Toshiba and IBM, two of the top brands in personal computers. In the PC market, Sony has little choice but to work with Microsoft Corp. and Palm Inc., because those are the two most widely accepted operational system standards. Yet, in the games business, Sony competes fiercely with Microsoft, as it does with Palm in the handheld-organizer market. In the end, what these various mutations of alliances reflect is a new and rapidly emerging reality about business today: that companies often have more to gain from love — or at least peaceful coexistence — than from war.

TO COLLABORATE OR COMPETE?

Why collaborate when you can compete?

The simple answer: Necessity. Cooperation can be a low-cost route for new competitors to gain technology and market access almost instantaneously. It takes so much money nowadays to develop new products and new technology and to penetrate new markets that few companies can really go it alone in every situation. A strategic alliance can potentially strengthen all participants against outsiders, even though it may at the same time weaken the partners against one another. But the bottom line is this: alliances can essentially provide short-cuts for companies to improve production efficiency and quality control and reach new consumers around the globe.

In the automobile industry, for example, these collaborative relationships are clear-cut. Each of the Big Three U.S. companies has alliance relationships that cross national boundaries. GM, for example, has alliances with Toyota Motor Corp., Isuzu Motors Inc., and Suzuki Motors Corp., as well as Daewoo Motor Co., in which GM is a shareholder. Ford's main alliances are with Mazda Motor Corp. and Kia Motors Corp. Chrysler, which had terminated a similar relationship with Mitsubishi Motors Corp. several years earlier, took a giant step beyond alliance in mid 1998, and shocked the world with the announcement that it planned to merge with Daimler-Benz of Germany to form a company called DaimlerChrysler. But the merger made sense. Each of the two companies had serious gaps in its geographical coverage and model lineup; together, they expected to plug each other's gaps, and become a strong full-line global competitor.

In the high-technology industries where Sony competes, the same phenomenon of "co-opetition" is apparent. Alliances have proliferated, often out of sheer necessity. Gone are the days when companies could survive on stand-alone gadgets or could distinguish themselves from others on the mere merits of a superior technology. Each company in the high-tech sector now faces the challenges of rapid change and a high degree of uncertainty. The lightening-speed regeneration and refinement of technology is draining the resources of companies that try to keep up with every one of the technologies. Because of this, alliances make necessary sense in the high-tech sector. The kinds of alliances within this sector can vary widely in the number of participants and the nature of the relationship. But nearly all are motivated by the same three goals: to increase global market access and market share; to acquire new technologies or exploit complementary ones; and to source products through supplier relationships.

Strategic alliances are ultimately tricky to manage because the companies involved in the alliance have to recognize that ultimately collaboration is competition in a different form. No collaboration is timeless. So it is a matter of how the companies within the alliance go about guarding their most valuable information while working together. Dutch electronics giant, Royal Philips Electronics, and Sony, an alliance we will discuss in greater depth later in this chapter, worked together to set a standard for compact-disc technology. But their research teams eventually went separate ways to develop more sophisticated technology for the compact disk including recordable functions. The Sony-Philips collaboration is a good case study of how the collaboration worked to their mutual benefit and delicately balanced the challenges of protecting proprietary information while working together.

"NOT INVENTED HERE" ATTITUDE

Up until the 1980s, Sony thrived on making stand-alone gadgets — the Walkman, Betamax (despite its eventual failure), and the Trinitron color television, to name a few — that were smarter and more sophisticated than those of its competitors. The success of Sony's audio-visual business gave it the confidence to feel superior to all others. In a way, though, this same success was also responsible for what one Sony executive calls a "not invented here" syndrome — the idea that if it's not invented by Sony, it's not good enough.

The damage this can cause was made more than evident by the Betamax project we discussed earlier.

What became clear from this episode, and what caused the company to lose out to JVC in the battle for video-tape supremacy, was that Sony's engineers were too focused on the sophistication of their own machinery to see that the length of recording time the tape allowed was also important to consumers.

Sony would lose again 15 years later, this time to Toshiba, in the standards war that raged around the product now known as DVD, digital video disc. Sony and Phillips, its partner in developing DVD technology, broke ranks with a consumer-electronics industry consortium that had agreed on certain standards for licensing and making the DVD, registering a patent instead for their own technology. In the end, the Toshiba technology, though more cumbersome, won out because it allowed more storage space and more flexibility as to the future evolution of the DVD.

> **"We now have to be more flexible and realize that we can use other people's resources for our own benefit." — Sony executive**

There is no one defining moment to mark when Sony realized that it would no longer be able to go at it alone. But certainly, the 1990s were not too kind to Sony. In one market after another — films, PCs, mobile communications — Sony was suddenly looking lackluster. Even Sony Computer Entertainment Inc., the video-game unit that spawned the mighty PlayStation, now faced formidable competition from Microsoft and its souped-up XBox. The VAIO computer has made little impact in the European and U.S. markets, where consumers' price-conscious purchasing behavior often discouraged them from buying a VAIO. Although the computer did offer good value for its price compared to competitors, giving consumers sophisticated audio and visual editing tools, it didn't draw the mass-audience users it was targeting. In 1999, Sony gave up an alliance with mobile-phone maker Qualcomm Inc. and left the U.S. market after the PCS mobile telecommunications standard it chose failed to generate much enthusiasm from consumers.

In recent years, Sony has found itself in an increasingly crowded field of makers of low-cost but high-quality electronics. Its rivals have an advantage in that there are increasing numbers of standard technologies that they can buy, helping to level the playing field and allow them to bring products to market quickly. In the past, Sony had used technology to its advantage, pioneering technology formats — the compact disc, for instance — that brought it licensing fees in addition to product sales. While these days aren't over, a growing number of technologies that Sony uses, such as the Windows operating system and the MP3 music compression format, are either owned by someone else or are available free of charge. Either way, Sony doesn't have an edge anymore. The global slump in consumer electronics in the last two years and dwindling profit margins are forcing Sony to re-evaluate its innovation philosophy.

As one Sony executive puts it: "It's not that we're giving up our innovative spirit. We will still strive to create new technologies and pioneer as we've always striven to do. But we now have to be more flexible and realize that we can use other people's resources for our own benefit. When Sony was still a simple audio-visual company, we often suffered from a "not invented here" syndrome. It's no longer a good idea to stick to that mentality."

RACING AGAINST TIME, WORKING WITH OTHERS

Notwithstanding the "not invented here" syndrome, Sony has enjoyed some success from allying itself with other corporations to develop technology. After the Betamax experience, Sony perhaps learned that it would need the support of others in the industry in order to push through technology that it initiated to become the standard in the industry. By linking with others, gathering competitors' strengths to complement its own, Sony could share the risks and, sometimes, the finances that are involved in stepping into entirely new business realms.

It was largely for this reason that Sony's co-founders first linked up with CBS Records Inc. in a joint venture in Japan, before eventually buying the record label in 1988. Sony's development of the tape recorder created a need for music that could be played on the machine. It believed that a tight partnership with a record label would give it access to the music that would spark users' interest in purchasing a tape recorder.

But in examining Sony's history of collaboration, there is perhaps no better case study and no more successful joint venture than its partnership with Philips to set the standard for compact-disc technology. The partnership was mutually beneficial. Sony's privileged access to music through CBS/ Sony Records generated a competitive advantage for the partners' technology. Philips' early understanding of how to make the disc small in size but generous in recording memory was a large part of why the Sony-Philips technology was widely accepted by most electronics manufacturers.[2]

Even before Sony and Philips engineers started exchanging know-how in 1979, the two companies had already tried individually to develop their own digital recording devices. By 1974, Philips had already incorporated a laser in an early video laser disc. For its part, Sony had also made a machine capable of digital recording, but it was the size of a refrigerator and weighed several hundred pounds. Subsequently, the Sony team was able to devise a processor that would permit digital signals to be recorded on tape and would play back the recording on a U-Matic three-quarter-inch player. This system was still unwieldy and had its own technical problems, but when it was performing optimally, it managed to deliver a clarity of sound that could not be retrieved from analog signals.

By the late 1970s, the musically trained Norio Ohga, then an executive deputy vice-president at Sony, was already enamored of digital recording, which he had likened to "removing a heavy winter coat from the sound". When he learned that an audio laser disc was in development, he ordered it to be brought to completion as a top priority, regardless of the cost.

A principal reason for Ohga's excitement about creating a new standard in the recording business was the opportunity it would create to combine new hardware with the rich "software" holdings of CBS/Sony Records. But most Sony audio engineers, having grown up in the analog age, were immovably convinced that analog sound was the genuine article. The manager of the project, Neitaro Nakajima, would later be given credit for pushing forward in typical Sony fashion in the face of internal skepticism to establish the company's future in digital sound. Later, listening to the system after it had been refined, Sony co-founder Masaru Ibuka would eventually acknowledge the digital sound system's superiority to the Tape-corder, a product of his era, but he would never express particular admiration for the digital technology that allowed for the crisper sound.

By the spring of 1976, Sony engineers were only able to present to Ohga an audio-laser disc 30 centimeters across, the size of an LP record, a musical "platter" with a capacity of 13 hours and 20 minutes of digital sound. While this was undoubtedly a step in the right direction, the disc was hard to manufacture and would end up costing the record company more than $1 million to produce each disc.

In the spring of 1979, Philips' chief audio engineer traveled to Japan to demonstrate its variation of the optical laser disc to Sony and other electronics manufacturers. The Philips prototype was 11.5 centimeters across and could hold an hour of digital information. Although one faction within the Dutch electronics giant had been inclined to choose Matsushita Electric Industrial Corp., Sony's biggest rival, as a partner, Wisse Dekker, who was now president, and Johan Van Tilberg, head of Philips' audio group, were both Sony admirers and cast the decisive votes in Sony's favor.

From August 1979 until June 1980, when they presented their standards to the Digital Audio Disc Conference — a consortium of 29 manufacturers drawn together with a view to achieving standardization — Sony and Philips' physicists and audio engineers alternated visits to one another's laboratories in Tokyo and Eindhoven. As technical problems surfaced, each team addressed them separately. The solutions were tested and compared at the next meeting. Working to a tight 10-month deadline for completion, the atmosphere was competitive. Each side was vying to end up with more patents in the finished product and there were heated arguments over the size and thickness of the compact disc and the number of recording hours it would allow.

As the optical disc research evolved, debate focused on two main issues. One was the number of bits, the units of digital memory, which ultimately determined the quality of the sound; Philips maintained that 14 bits would be sufficient. But Sony argued that 16 bits, though more costly and complex, would help distinguish their product from competing systems in development. The second issue related to size and capacity: Philips proposed an 11.5-centimeter disc, which would fit into a car audio system in the European market, and would allow a recording capacity of 60 minutes. Ohga was adamantly opposed on the grounds that a 60-minute limit was "unmusical". At that length, the musically trained Ohga pointed out, a single disc could not accommodate all of Beethoven's Ninth Symphony and would require interrupting many of the major operas before the end of the first act. On the other hand, 75 minutes would accommodate most important pieces of music, at least to a place where it made musical sense to cut them. At 16 bits, the disc would have to measure 12 centimeters to accommodate Ohga's proposed recording length. In the end, Philips agreed to Sony's specifications.

At the final session of the first round of research, held in Tokyo in March 1980, the two teams tested one another's error-correction systems on discs that had been scratched, marked with fingerprints and dusted with chalk. The Philips system proved inadequate to meet these extreme demands, and Sony was judged the winner. But, later, Ohga and Nakajima would decide to agree that the CD technology should be considered an equal contribution from both sides.

As early as September 1977, 29 manufacturers from around the world had formed the Digital Audio Disc (DAD) Conference with an eye to achieving standardization. In June 1980, in Salzburg, DAD reviewed three systems: Sony and Philips' optical system; a mechanical system developed by Telefunken; and an electro-static system that belonged to JVC. In April 1981, DAD announced that it was endorsing both the Sony-Philips and the JVC systems. JVC was a subsidiary of Matsushita, Sony's long-time rival, which Sony engineers largely blamed for driving Betamax out of business. In this instance, however, Sony would get a happy ending. The superiority of the Sony-Philips approach — the laser read the information without any physical contact with the surface of the disc — and Sony's privileged access to music through CBS/Sony Records would generate a competitive advantage for Sony. Before long, most electronics manufacturers around the world had joined the Sony-Philips camp and were licensing their technology.

It is conceivable that Sony's audio engineers eventually could have developed a similarly sophisticated CD technology on their own. But under the circumstances at the time, in a fierce race with JVC and other developers to set the CD standard, Sony's best bet was to work with Philips.

DISCOVER NEW WORLDS WITH PARTNERS

In 1986, when Sony made its first attempt to enter the Japanese computer market, the company again looked for a jumpstart through partners.

The plan was to create a multimedia home computer, and Nobuyuki Idei, now the chairman of Sony Corporation, organized a collaboration that was to include Sony, Philips, Apple Computer Inc. and Microsoft. The project fell apart for reasons that were largely out of Sony's control, when Wayne Rosing, the project's champion at Apple, was fired by Steve Jobs. Subsequently, Idei's group at Sony designed the MSX, a home computer that used MSX Basic and was driven by a Motorola chip. Idei was in charge of launching the machine, but was unable to win market share because the machine didn't distinguish itself sufficiently from what was already available on the marketplace. So, in 1991, Sony withdrew its MSX products from the Japanese markets.

Despite its initial failure, Sony continued to seek partners to assist its entry into the PC business. It became quite clear in the mid 1990s that the profit margins for the consumer-electronics business were diminishing quickly. The beginning of the end of stand-alone gadgets had begun. The advent of the Internet opened the consumer-electronics industry to cross-industry competitors, and Sony desperately wanted a piece of the expanding home-PC market. In November 1995, Sony and Intel Corp. announced a joint venture dubbed "the GI Project" — after Intel's chairman Andy Grove and Idei — in which Intel would manufacture chips for a Microsoft Windows-based personal computer. At the time, although Sony possessed CD-Rom storage technology and manufactured monitor displays, there was no computer project in development. Idei was certain of the PC's importance in Sony's value chain, and was pushing aggressively for Sony to work with Intel to develop their own line of personal computers. In April 1996, he increased the pressure by creating an information technology group within Sony. For the first year, the new company, headed by Kunitake Ando (now president of Sony Corp.), marketed a standard mini-tower desktop machine built with Intel, while its engineers scrambled to design a thoroughgoing Sony product. In July 1997, the VAIO line of mini-tower desktops and a laptop was released in Japan and became a huge hit.

Sony's attempt to enter the computer market with VAIO was far more successful than previous attempts for obvious reasons: it used what it understood most — consumer behavior — and coupled it with what its partner, Intel, knew the best — making quality processing chips — to create a different kind of computer that would be an entertainment center rather than a white box with word processing for the workplace. Using Intel know-how, Sony combined the technology with its keen understanding of consumer needs and wants to create a different kind of machine, one that would be geared towards video, photo and music editing, rather than towards pure word processing and data-entry purposes. In this, Intel and Sony found in one another complementary qualities that made the working relationship smooth and mutually beneficial.

COMMITMENT COUNTS

While the Sony-Philips alliance is a perfect example of successful collaboration, Sony's alliance with Ericsson to develop the mobile-phone market illustrates some of the challenges alliances can pose. The joint venture is still more of a disappointment than a success story — at least for now. Founded in October, 2001, the Sony Ericsson alliance missed its target of becoming profitable within its first year. Although its first-quarter sales of US$107 million were encouraging, the second quarter experienced losses of nearly US$90 million.

Sony and Ericsson have both operated loss-making mobile-phone units for quite some years. Ericsson, despite its large scale and once being ranked number two in mobile phones in the late 1990s, faced a host of problems on handsets, including clumsy design, speed to market and branding. Sony had a small global market share, with little penetration beyond its own borders. The hope in marrying the two companies through a 50-50 joint venture was to leverage Ericsson's radio know-how and combine it with Sony's expertise in consumer electronics, branding and marketing and its knowledge of the games and entertainment areas, all crucial for mobile Internet development. In short, the joint venture equals engineers plus salesmen, which seemed like a good plan, on the surface.[3]

Sony Ericsson's goal is lofty: to be the number-one worldwide multimedia terminal provider five years from now, overtaking Nokia Corp., currently the leading mobile-phone provider. The vision was to develop phones with wireless gaming capabilities and content-delivery functions through SMS (short messaging service), MMS (multimedia messaging service) and Sony Ericsson's Bluetooth wireless technologies. The alliance was supposed to reduce the cost base of mobile-phone manufacturing and to increase the market share of both companies. Despite the success of the T68 tri-band color handset, Sony Ericsson has yet to make a dent in the marketplace. The global slump in mobile phones is part of the reason for this and, despite the strength of the Sony name and Ericsson's distribution network in Europe, Sony Ericsson has achieved neither the strong brand recognition that Nokia enjoys nor the cost competitiveness that Samsung has.

But putting aside the slump in the global telecommunications industry, one of the key challenges facing the Sony Ericsson alliance is commitment — on the part of Ericsson, that is. For Ericsson, selling handsets is only a minor part of its business. Its core business of telecommunications infrastructure has been floundering in the midst of the global slump. In a press conference in 2002, Ericsson chief

Sony Ericsson T68i mobile phone — Courtesy of Sony Ericsson

executive officer Kurt Hellstrom, who also serves as chairman of Sony Ericsson, warned of the possibility of Ericsson leaving the joint venture, but later rephrased this to say that it was watching the joint venture cautiously. For Sony, the stakes are much higher — mobile phones and the wireless realm are a key part of Sony's four networked platforms. The venture should have given it the global access to the European market that it didn't have as a stand-alone business unit.

The joint-venture ride has been bumpy so far. In July 2002, Sony Ericsson canceled the production of Z700 phones, which featured a color screen and more advanced games, because consumers wanted cheaper phones. Analysts covering the mobile-technology sector say that Sony Ericsson will have to come out with more low-end products if they want to compete with Nokia and Motorola Inc. whose products cater to the wide range of consumers that Sony Ericsson wants to capture. There are high-end phones with fancy functions and technology for the sophisticated user, but Nokia and Motorola have both introduced cheaper cellular phones to cater to price-conscious consumers amid cooling economies worldwide. Despite once being a leading handset vendor, Sony Ericsson now has only one-third of Motorola's market share, as second-quarter 2002 numbers indicate. (Motorola has 15.7 per cent market share versus Sony Ericssons' 5.4 per cent. In the corresponding period the previous year, Sony Ericsson had 7.7 per cent.)

More recently, Sony has tapped synergies within its businesses to push its phones. In May 2002, to coincide with the premiere of Sony Pictures Entertainment's blockbuster, *Spider-Man*, Sony Ericsson teamed up with U.S. wireless-phone service provider Cingular to introduce the T68, which carried a Spiderman image on the cover. In Sony movies, too, there has been a conscious attempt to display Sony Ericsson phones to generate consumer interest. But so far, with delays in new model launches, Sony Ericsson is still far behind its main rivals. Until it is able to capture the hearts of price-conscious users, it may not be able to realize the kind of short-term profits it had hoped for. Right now, Sony and Ericsson officials have renewed commitment to the joint venture, banking on the introduction of color model T300, targeted to a mass audience, to appeal more to cost-conscious consumers.[4]

Despite the disappointments to date, analysts say that it's still too early to give a final verdict on the fate of the Sony Ericsson joint venture. Was this particular alliance a bad move on either corporation's part? Probably not. It would have been difficult for Sony to go at the mobile-phone business alone, with its limited experience in wireless technologies and of the mobile-phone industry. It would have been hard, even with Sony's marketing and consumer-electronics expertise, to snatch market share from the likes of Nokia, Samsung and Motorola. Other mobile-phone vendors are watching cautiously to see how the Sony Ericsson alliance develops. It is, analysts say, a potentially formidable threat to the position of other vendors. But, of course, that reality has yet to be realized.

Some analysts have argued that if Ericsson does step away from the alliance, this would ultimately benefit Sony. Sony could then acquire a majority stake in the joint venture, and be the driving force behind the partnership, injecting into it the spirit of marketing and innovation on which the Sony reputation is founded. But some academics suggest that sometimes managers are too obsessed with ownership structure when they should focus on creating synergies that would leverage each company's strengths. And there is something to be said for this: collaboration may sometimes be unavoidable; surrender is not.

THE SONY-NOKIA PARTNERSHIP

Who says competitors can't work together, even in the same industry?

Sony and Finnish mobile giant Nokia announced in November 2001 that they will cooperate to develop an open and common middleware platform. This would allow mobile handsets and various consumer-electronics devices to have inter-operability, the ability to exchange information, and a common platform that would make their respective service platforms compatible.

The focus of the collaboration is on a number of key technologies that will enable communication between various types of gadgets and handsets, allowing them to utilize applications and software over the network. The collaboration will cover technical areas such as new user-interfaces, content downloading, multimedia messaging, and open digital-rights management, among other issues.

The partnership, analysts say, has been driven largely by a need to create some standards for the mobile world that will enable users on different mobile systems to communicate with one another. As people become more reliant on their mobile phones, the compatibility of phones from different manufacturers becomes more important. The collaboration will combine Nokia's expertise in mobile communications with Sony's experience in technical innovation and creating games and entertainment to set industry standards for handset compatibility.

In a press release announcing the joint venture, Jorma Ollila, chairman and CEO of Nokia, laid out the path the companies would follow: "Nokia and Sony share a vision of a future in which many types of devices work together exchanging data and content in a seamless and interoperable way. This is a task that requires broad and open interoperability between devices from many manufacturers. I am confident that this cooperation with Sony will significantly promote the target of merging different service environments together. Nokia's mission is to enable people to build their own mobile world."[5]

INEVITABLE PARTNERSHIPS

Most partnerships are initiated out of a mutual need to survive. In the case of Sony and Ericsson or in the case of Sony and Philips, the drive to form alliances originated from the belief that the two companies could benefit and complement one another in the quest to enter new markets and reach more consumers.

> "We used to try to do everything by ourselves. But now we've changed our attitude 100 per cent. Now it's very important that we have a good alliance with AOL … although we may compete in other areas." —
> Kunitake Ando,
> Sony president

But sometimes partners are born out of sheer necessity, simply because these corporations that Sony allies itself with are absolutely crucial to its quest to expand into new business realms. In this regard, Sony has focused largely on software providers that will enable interactive linkage between the home portal and network services. With Howard Stringer, chairman of Sony Corporation of America, acting as the intermediary, Sony has been able to maintain ongoing dialogues with Microsoft, Sun Microsystems, Cisco Systems Inc. and other members of "the community".

The dialogue has led to a series of licensing agreements for software applications. In March 1998, Sony licensed "personaljava" technology from Sun Microsystems for use in the home-entertainment network environment it is developing at its new Software Platform Development Center. The following month, Microsoft and Sony announced plans to cross-license Microsoft's Windows CE, an operating system for digital consumer-electronics products, and Sony's Home Networking Module, a "middleware", which allows digital "appliances" to be interconnected and interoperated. "The time has come," Idei declared at a press conference with Bill Gates, "for the PC industry and the AV industry to shake hands." Then, in July, Sony licensed its Home Networking

Module to General Instrument, Inc., for use in its digital "set-top devices", the transformed cable boxes that are expected to function as a primary home gateway to digital interactive services.[6]

In June 2002, Sony invested US$20 million to acquire a 6 per cent minority stake in Palm Inc.'s subsidiary PalmSource, the company in charge of overseeing and upgrading Palm's operating system for handheld organizers. Sony has been a licensee of the Palm operating system since 1999, and uses it for the Clié handheld organizer. In a reciprocal move, the collaboration allowed Palm to incorporate Sony's Memory Stick technology into its operating system. The collaboration was an attempt to help popularize Sony's technology which, to date, is still limited to Sony devices and a few other agreements of this sort. With the equity stake Sony has taken in PalmSource, Sony has signaled its intention to extend its relationship with Palm to develop upgraded platforms for the Clié handheld.[7]

AOL-SONY ALLIANCE

At Comdex in Las Vegas in 1999, Sony introduced a new strategy for Idei's networked world vision: a ubiquitous value-network concept in which devices and products can access the network seamlessly and connect with each other at any time, from any place. The deal will see AOL provide online content, Web browser, instant messaging system and access to 31 million subscribers. The collaboration to develop a Web browser will challenge the current industry leaders, Netscape and Microsoft's Internet Explorer. As part of the deal with AOL and Sony, Nokia will release some of its middleware and service software, while Sony will contribute its hardware expertise and digital-rights management technology. The plan is to give almost all consumers' electronic devices seamless and wireless broadband network access at speeds of up to five gigabits per second.

AOL Time Warner competes directly with Sony in the movie-making business. But as Kunitake Ando, president of Sony Corporation puts it: "We used to try to do everything by ourselves. But now we've changed our attitude 100 per cent; 180 degrees actually. Now it's very important that we have a good alliance with AOL...although we may compete in other areas."

WAIT, WHY COLLABORATE?

There is no doubt this new business era of alliances and partnerships has triggered some unease about the long-term consequences. Do alliances among groups of firms signal the end of competition or the reduction of competition within or across industries? As we have seen from Sony's involvements with the likes of Philips, Palm and Microsoft, using an alliance with a competitor to acquire new technologies or skills can, in fact, be beneficial for both parties. Such alliances reflect the commitment and capacity of each partner to absorb the skills of the other. But what is absolutely crucial to a sound alliance/partnership is strategic intent, the essential ingredient in the commitment to mutual learning. For collaboration to succeed, each partner must contribute something distinctive: basic research, product development skills, manufacturing capacity, access to distribution. From Sony's end, its typical strengths — marketing, branding and a sophisticated understanding of consumer behavior — make it an attractive candidate for other companies to partner with. These are precisely the things that attracted Philips and Ericsson. In the end, each party to such an alliance wants to emerge from it more competitive than when it entered. With Sony Ericsson, this will depend largely on whether Ericsson comes through with a solid commitment. Whether Sony Ericsson will be able to grab market share from Nokia and Motorola remains to be seen.

In the case of the Sony/Philips' collaboration in compact-disc technology, winning the standardization war over JVC and other competitors helped push Sony's CD Discman and, later on, its digital video-disc research along. The CD had lacked a player equal to the disc's potential, and creating an acceptable CD player at an affordable price became the challenge for Sony. On October 1, 1982, Sony introduced to the Japanese market its first CD player, the CDP 101. At the same time, CBS/Sony Records released the world's first 50 CD titles. There was some jazz and some pop, including Billy Joel's *52nd Street*, but the catalog was weighted toward masterworks from the classical canon, reflecting Ohga's judgment that classical music fans would better appreciate the benefits of digital recording.

The launch generated excitement, but the first CD player was priced prohibitively at ¥168,000 (roughly US$700): once audiophiles willing to pay any price had been skimmed from the top of the market, sales began to lag. By November 1984, the second anniversary of the CD, Sony had developed a new player, the D-50, which was half the size and one-third the price of the original. Today, Sony Discmans are a tremendous success, thanks largely to the Sony/Philips partnership that set the standard for digital sound recording.

SONY'S RECIPES FOR SUCCESS

- *Put away past animosities*: Today's world no longer has much room for old rivalries. Even the oldest of enemies are beginning to work with one another to keep up with the changing global business community. Look for and seize new opportunities when they come around with both current and former friends and foes.

- *Discover new worlds with partners*: Beyond mere corporate survival, partnerships are a sure way to keep up with changing technologies and the burgeoning wealth of information available in the world.

- *Be committed to your partners*: Joint ventures and partnerships often fail because of a lack of commitment. To explore new markets requires a certain level of dedication from all partners. So be true to your word and commit to partnerships that are worthwhile.

- *Make the best of being big*: Size no longer confers upon its possessors the advantages that it used to offer implicitly. Still, size could work to your advantage as large corporations have more resources and more diversified businesses, and could see a wider range of new opportunities and partners to help your company continue to grow.

NOTES

1. Marina Whitman, "New World, New Rules: From Global Dominance to Global Competition", *Harvard Business School Working Knowledge*, March 7, 2000.

2. Nathan, op. cit.

3. Christopher Brown-Humes and Michiyo Nakamoto, "Sony and Ericsson put on a show of unity: The groups' mobile joint venture is fighting to gain market share", *The Financial Times*, September 13, 2002.

4. Kyoko Suzuki, "Sony President Ando Comments on Handset Venture with Ericsson", *Bloomberg News*, September 4, 2002.

5. Sony corporate website www.sony.net.

6. Yuri Kageyama, "Getting gadgets online a pillar of new Sony strategy", *Associated Press*, January 13, 2002.

7. "Palm rises as Sony deal helps towards goal to spin off PalmSource", *AFX Asia*, October 9, 2002.

Further information in this chapter is taken from interviews with Kei Sakaguchi, Masanobu Sakaguchi, Mack Araki, Susan Tick and Don Levy, Sony employees in the U.S. and Japan.

Ten

REINVENTING FOR A NETWORKED FUTURE

Imagine a future with a personal computer shaped like an egg that knows all your wants and needs. Or a computer with "little eyes" that can sense your moods or feed conversation material at cocktail parties. This chapter gives a glimpse of what lies ahead in Sony's future.

At Sony DreamWorld 2002 in Yokohama in September, Sony showcased its vision of the digital future with new conceptual models of what its VAIO computers might look like two years from now. The showcase was the chance for Sony to finally explain visually what its chairman, Nobuyuki Idei, had been describing for almost five years as the Age of Networks, and gave some concrete backing for Idei's self-coined term "digital dream kid".

Take the Content Egg for example. A flat, egg-shaped "personal server", this futuristic VAIO stores a user's important data and can send the data to a notebook PC on the move, via the Internet, whenever and wherever the user requests it. It is designed to be portable, so users can take the "egg" anywhere with them and still access information they need. Another prototype is the VAIO E.Q., a compact hexagonal "sensing computer", which has the ability to store data such as still images and voice memos, memorize the user's preferences and personal information, and act as the wireless interface between the user and any intelligent device, including perhaps robots. For example, at a cocktail party, the future VAIO could "see" an approaching person's face, scour a database and match the face to a name fast enough to help its owner avoid embarrassment. In a way, these next-generation VAIOs will have "little eyes", sensing cameras that could learn their owners' experiences and become their personal agents.

Welcome to the networked future — or at least the one that Sony is trying to sell to consumers. This is Sony's plan for reinventing its image, transforming itself from a consumer-electronics giant into a broadband entertainment company in the digital era. The analog era was good to Sony, with inventions such as Walkmans, Trinitron televisions and transistor radios becoming widely popular and profitable for their times. But in the digital era, the company has had to shift gears. Manufacturing electronics hardware has become increasingly less profitable both because of competition from lower-cost manufacturers in Asia, and because of the spread and influence of the Internet, which has fundamentally changed consumer behavior. With the advent of this digital era, Sony has proposed a new plan for its future: the digitization of the company, in which all of its hardware and content would be able to communicate with one another. The company foresees consumers using its networked products to gain access to a range of content and services anytime, anywhere.

If Sony succeeds in realizing this dream, tomorrow's Sony will no longer resemble today's consumer-electronics powerhouse, just as today's Sony is a sharp contrast to the tiny radio-repair shop hidden in a bombed-out department store in post-war Tokyo. But if Sony guesses wrong — if it overestimates the consumers' appetite for music, videos and games delivered digitally on everything from television sets to mobile phones — it risks losing a competitive edge against rivals ranging from Nokia to Samsung to Microsoft. This is perhaps the biggest gamble Sony has undertaken since co-founder Akio Morita pushed the company into Hollywood more than a decade ago. And this time around, it is no longer just a reputation that is at stake. It is the entire company's financial well-being.

CREATING THE SONY NETWORK

Since Idei assumed leadership at Sony in 1995, he has been trying aggressively to paint a picture of the "new Sony" — one whose ambitions lie in broadband entertainment. Calling himself the Digital Dream Kid, Idei wants the company to move in the direction of connectivity in which Sony's products — mobile phones, digital cameras, televisions, multimedia computers, game consoles, portable stereos, video recorders, set-top boxes, handheld organizers, even robots — can all access the Internet or an Internet gateway device and "talk" to one another. Once all these products are connected, Idei envisions that Sony will be able to deliver music, movies, television, games, and data services to customers wherever they may be; in the office, at home, in the car, or wandering down the street. At a demonstration at Sony's Media World, an invitation-only showroom in Shinagawa, Tokyo, customers can take digital pictures or videos on their mobile phone, press the send button, either via email or Bluetooth wireless technology, and instantly see them show up on a personal computer or a photo printer.

But grand and creative as Idei's vision of a new Sony might be, executing the strategy will be trying. For a company that has adamantly insisted on creating the appetite for consumers, convincing consumers to buy this network vision will be a daunting task, particularly since the majority of consumers have been slow to embrace high-speed networks, and technologies are changing more rapidly now than in the analog era. It is both harder to predict consumer behavior, and harder to predict market trends. Selling the vision to dealers will also be difficult because it could mean that the retailers will have to actually reconceive and reconfigure their stores to accommodate the new Sony products.

Today, most electronics stores are organized along the lines of the products they carry: Camcorders in one section; PCs in another; and TVs against a back wall. Digital cameras and mobile devices are usually in the front of the store, DVD players and video recorders on the side. In this segregated design, it's almost impossible to illustrate to and educate consumers on the benefits of networked devices such as Airboard, a wireless portable video and Internet display that could serve as both a television and a computer, or a Cocoon, a "channel server" device for recording television shows and streaming them to the personal computer. Sony has begun offering consumer seminars in Japan to educate retailers on how to sell the networked products. But the campaign to educate consumers is much easier in Japan, where manufacturers are allowed to display their products prominently according to their own design. For example, the VAIO computer section at a Tokyo electronics store would feature the trademark silvery purple color of the computer, and would include loud, large signs directing consumers to the section. But in the U.S. and Europe, manufacturers have little say in how their products would be displayed with respect to their competitors'. Products are lined up according to category without much fanfare. Sony marketers in the U.S. say they have discussed different alternatives with retailers on how they could create product displays that could more easily demonstrate the potential of these networked gadgets. Even though Sony's American marketers say they are making some progress, realistically, to succeed in the U.S. and Europe, Sony would have to either persuade retailers to reconfigure their stores — a highly unlikely prospect — or decide to develop more of their own retail-selling environments along the lines of the Sony showrooms in New York and Tokyo.

Retailing challenges aside, Sony still has to convince its own executives that this network vision is the right path for the company. Historically, Sony's business units have pursued their goals and strategies largely independently. Hardware and content managers, for example, are literally oceans and continents apart, with the electronics wizards and game developers in Japan, the moviemakers in California, and the music makers in New York. The companies may fall under the same parent umbrella, but they have widely different management philosophies that often are defined by the cultures of their industries or their geographical locations. Sony executives in the different business units admit to this cultural gap. As detailed in previous chapters, differences in cultures of the businesses have, in the past, caused rifts and tensions between the different business units, sometimes at the expense of the Sony group's overall financial health.

Since Idei assumed leadership, he has tried to create more cohesion within the group as a whole. First, he reshuffled the management at Sony Pictures Entertainment, bringing in movie industry veterans with a proven track record. He also revamped the power structure in the U.S., bringing in Sir Howard Stringer, a man with experience in both the entertainment and electronics businesses, to head Sony Corporation of America. Finally, he promoted Masayuki Nozoe, one of the company's few senior managers with experience in consumer electronics and in the music and movie groups, to head an initiative called the Network Application and Content Service Sector, or NACSS. Nozoe's mission is to do organizationally within Sony what Sony is striving to do in the market with its products — make everything work together seamlessly, bridging the businesses of hardware and content.

But if persuading consumers is a difficult task, closing the cultural and organizational gap between hardware and content units is an even more daunting project, particularly with valued Sony managers such as Ken Kutaragi wishing out loud in the media that his company, Sony Computer Entertainment, were independent again. Still, the mental shift is beginning to take place now, slowly but surely. "It took almost two years for everyone to grasp the network concept and go in the same direction," said Kunitake Ando, president of Sony, at the 2002 Sony DreamWorld showcase. "Now we're all going the same way. The horizontal and vertical are more balanced."

According to Sony executives, engineers no longer start work on a new device without considering how it will play on the network. And as we saw earlier, hardware and content managers now gather regularly for meetings and stay in touch via email and video-conferences. From these closer collaborations, software developed initially for Sony handhelds and computers has been adapted for use on the entertainment side to download movie trailers. There have been advertising campaigns that combine Sony movie characters with mobile phones and audio products such as the Walkman and the Discman. The collaborations are still by no means seamless, but at least it's a move in the right direction, Sony executives say.

DEFINING SONY'S PLACE IN THE DIGITAL FUTURE

Chasing the network vision brings Sony into conflict with daunting new adversaries that are more experienced in telecommunications and computing than it is. The digital world has brought Sony beyond the confines of consumer electronics. Media giants in the entertainment world, such as AOL Time Warner, are trying to develop the same one-stop-shop vision as Sony of becoming providers of content, services and online distribution. In an overly crowded consumer-electronics industry, which still accounts for nearly two-thirds of Sony's revenue, new competitors are rising to challenge Sony with cheaper high-quality goods, and old foes such as Matsushita and Philips are fighting fiercely for dwindling profits in the industry. With Microsoft, Intel, Apple and Samsung all pushing broadband visions of their own, Sony finds itself in a race against time to establish its broadband vision as the standard.

There is a lot riding on Sony being able to sell this network vision to the world. But it's hardly an easy time considering the global economic slump. Consumer confidence is at a nine-year low in the U.S., which is Sony's largest market, accounting for one-third of its sales. In Japan, the company's second-largest market, the economy has been in a recession for nearly a decade, with no relief in sight.

Still, there are reasons for Sony to be confident that it can still emerge an influential competitor in the broadband future. After a dismal fiscal 2001, in which profits fell 40 per cent, the company's margins are growing once again. Driving the rebound for the entire Sony group are cost-cutting programs, such as Project USA mentioned earlier in the book, that are already showing some effect, and brisk growth in products such as digital cameras and camcorders, big-screen TVs and computers, which have offset losses in music and mobile phones. Sony's desktop and laptop VAIO multimedia computers, for example, gained global market share faster than any other major PC brand, even though its market share in the U.S. and in European markets are still slim. Its PlayStation 2 game console has opened up a commanding lead over Microsoft's Xbox and Nintendo's Game Cube. (PlayStation accounted for more than half of Sony's $1 billion in profit in fiscal 2001, which ended March 31.) Thanks to *Spider-Man*, the Vin Diesel action film *XXX* and *Men In Black II*, Sony's movie business raked in more money in 2002 than any other studio. This was only the second year that the Sony studio had been able to turn a profit, partly because of a change in its strategy for selecting movies. If the studio is able to sustain this kind of growth for the long term, then the business could take on greater significance, particularly with Idei's vision of broadband entertainment.

STAY AHEAD OF THE INNOVATION GAME

Sony's fate is riding largely on whether consumers will buy the company's network vision and spend their money on these network-enabled electronics products, which are just beginning to show up in Japan. Banking on the day when these broadband-connected gadgets will be in the hands of millions of consumers, Sony already has a portfolio of 1,000 digitized films, 33,000 hours of TV programming, and more than 500,000 songs ready to be pumped out to them.

A solid example of the new network-enabled design philosophy is Sony's Bluetooth Handicam camcorder. (Bluetooth is a wireless technology that allows data to be transmitted from one Bluetooth-enabled device to another without a fixed connection.) Working wirelessly with a Sony-Ericsson phone that is also Bluetooth-enabled, the camcorder lets users send videoclips and still images to friends immediately via email without passing through a PC. The camcorder also sends images wirelessly to a Sony photo printer or to an Airboard. Users can also browse the web and receive short email messages on the camcorder's inbuilt LCD screen. Sony has also recently added miniature digital cameras to its Clié handheld organizer and its VAIO palmtop computers. Sony Ericsson plans to introduce a mobile phone with a digital camera embedded. When equipped with wireless adapters that Sony believes will eventually become standard, these video-enabled devices will allow someone attending a wedding, say, to send live video of the ceremony to friends watching on their computer screens, TV monitors, Airboards, or mobile handsets.

Sony has been preparing for this day for decades. The foundation was first laid when Akio Morita and his protégé, Norio Ohga, expanded the company into the realm of entertainment, with acquisitions in the late 1980s of music and movie businesses in the U.S. Now, at the beginning of a new millennium, if the network vision is to be fully realized, it is crucial that Sony finds a way to bring its electronics hardware and content businesses more into sync. Even if the devices achieve total connectivity, it will still be vital that Sony's entertainment businesses provide enough good content and services to keep the consumers interested. Nowhere is this urgent inter-business collaboration more important, and yet so challenging for Sony to explain, than in a new product line called Cocoon, which was showcased at Sony's DreamWorld 2002 event. Cocoon is a "smart" gateway to the Internet, one that Sony hopes will change the way people consume video, music, and other products and services that the company is developing for broadband distribution.

Sony describes it as "the future of television" — indeed, if Cocoon catches on, it could eventually become as integral a part of the TV as the tuner is today.

The first Cocoon product, a "channel server" that went on sale in Japan in November 2002 for US$1,100, is a kind of personal video recorder, similar to the TiVo or ReplayTV box available in the U.S. for recording television shows and movies for subscribers. The Cocoon can store up to 15 hours of high-definition video or 100 hours of regular television. There is also the option to double Cocoon's capacity should consumers so choose. Like other real-time, hard-drive recorders, it lets viewers pause live programming, rewind, skip commercials, and perform other video tricks. Cocoon is also built to communicate over a home network with a VAIO or other brand of PC, and through a permanent broadband connection to the Internet. Hook up the machine that way, and you can program a recording session remotely from an office PC or from a Web-browsing mobile phone. Cocoon also has the artificial intelligence to "learn" what kind of shows the owner likes to watch, based on an onscreen questionnaire and an analysis of what the user records onto the hard disk. It then autonomously scans the network and records similar shows, creating, in effect, a personal TV channel. Because of its network connection, the Cocoon can be upgraded to offer new products and services as they emerge. Just imagine this: future Sony stereo systems in the Cocoon series that could scan music services on the Internet for new tunes according to your tastes and preferences. Sony Music might even be able to send samples from new artists to entice online music sales.

Cocoon-enabled TVs are an example of one of four categories of "gateway" products upon which Sony is basing its strategy.

(The others are the VAIO computer, the PlayStation 2 game console, and mobile devices.) The idea that gadgets can tailor themselves to their owner is a fundamental element of Sony's digital strategy. It has certainly shaped the development of prototypes of future PCs such as the VAIO Content Egg and the hexagonal "sensing computer" mentioned earlier.

Another key part of Sony's strategy could be the AIBO, its artificially intelligent robo-pet. Already the company's Digital Creatures Laboratory is working on two-legged robots, and Toshitada Doi, president of the laboratory, believes that robots may eclipse PCs in product growth worldwide in two or three decades. Already, the most advanced AIBO robots can recognize spoken commands, demonstrate programmed moods, and can pick out their owners' faces in a crowd.

Still, AIBO was designed largely as entertainment. Sony's next robot, code-named the SDR-4X, will act more as a companion than as a pet. The SDR-4X, which is expected to reach the market in a year or two, can best be described as the physical embodiment of Astro-Boy, a popular cartoon character of post-war Japan, that combined a young boy's brain in the body of a humanoid robot. In demonstrations, the two-foot-tall SDR-4X walks on two legs to a microphone, gestures gracefully, and begins speaking and singing in a sweet, high-pitched voice. It has two "eyes", which give it depth perception and the ability to calculate distances, and it can get back on its feet if it falls. Sony designers envision a day when these two-legged robots, connected to a home network, might remind elderly owners that it is time to take their medication, "sing" music as it streams from a home gateway, or act as a roving security guard whose eyes broadcast video over a remote network connection.

Still, Sony executives say that, despite the emphasis on network-based content and services, the company will not lose its focus on hardware, its original roots. In its research and development laboratories, engineers are already trying to refine some of Sony's staple products: a TV display not much thicker than a few sheets of paper; high-definition video projectors that turn entire walls into film screens, and "digital chopsticks" — a digital pointer that allows a user to pluck a file or image directly from a computer or wallboard display and deposit it on, say, the TV screeen at home, just as one would use chopsticks to move a piece of food from one plate to another.

Other corporations that have started to initiate a broadband entertainment vision have stumbled along, giving analysts pause as to whether the consumer market is ready to usher in all the sophistication and possibilities of the digital era with open arms. In many ways, because of its history and experience, Sony may have a competitive advantage against rivals such as Hewlett-Packard, Microsoft and Philips to make the transition to the broadband world and sell it effectively to consumers. It has established design centers that clearly understand how to design consumer products that are both sexy and functional. It has a proven global distribution system and is in constant contact with consumers. It has a deep understanding of networking technology and how to market it. The wireless-product unit has also had a string of hits including the Clié handheld device and VAIO notebook computers. The Sony-Ericsson unit is struggling financially, but some of its products, including the T68 tri-band color phone, have done well in the marketplace. Even business units that used to lock horns are slowly finding synergies. When Sony's game developers develop a new product, it is now tailored not just for the PlayStation 2 but also for Sony

Cliés and Sony-Ericsson phones. Sony Pictures Entertainment software engineers think about how to develop content services compatible with Sony computers and handhelds. Sony designers even retooled the Walkman to integrate with VAIO PCs and Sony Music's Pressplay joint-venture online music service.

From all of these accomplishments, Sony does seem set to embrace this networked future. But, not so fast.

The biggest, and probably the most crucial, piece still missing from the broadband network puzzle is the network itself. In Sony's largest consumer market, the United States, broadband penetration will only reach 30 per cent by the end of 2005. For Sony's vision of a networked future to work, the company cannot do without broadband. A large part of the company's revenues will, it hopes, be derived from the digital distribution of music, video, games and other services. But with most Americans still getting Internet access through slower dial-up phone lines that are inhospitable to video and music, can Sony afford to wait for it to arrive?

This is the first time in Sony's history that it is making products that are ahead of the infrastructure's ability to use them, one analyst explained. When they came out with the first transistor radios and Trinitron TVs, the broadcasters were already there. When they came out with the Walkman, everyone was already using cassettes. There's a huge question mark over broadband networks, and whether consumers will be ready for what Sony has to offer. Undoubtedly, broadband will eventually become mainstream in the United States. But Sony will need to find alternative sources of revenue to keep the momentum going until its broadband networked vision is entirely realized.

For now, most analysts say, Sony still has some insulation from total risk. It can probably derive revenues from enough areas such as its gaming unit to fill the profit gaps for the short term. But that assumes, of course, that Sony can come up with broadband-ready products that consumers find compelling. The company has tried to test out the market at home in Japan first. More than half of all households there are expected to have broadband Internet access by the end of 2005. So products such as the Airboard and Cocoon, as well as new Cliés and VAIOs, are being tried in the Japanese market, where consumers are typically more enthused about gadgets than price-conscious consumers elsewhere. But as experience has proven, convincing consumers to stray from the stand-alone era of electronics gadgets isn't easy. The networked Walkman was a big hit in Japan but hasn't taken off in the U.S. Even Japanese consumers could not be easily swayed by the stylish but technically flawed eVilla, Sony's first attempt at an Internet appliance, released in 2001.

The Airboard, a favorite among Sony executives, has received only lukewarm responses even from consumers in Japan. As one Sony executive said: "Consumers don't quite know what to make of it. They don't understand whether it's a television or a computer or what. I think we have to do some more education with consumers." Sony executives are hoping that with Microsoft and other computer manufacturers working to introduce tablet computers, Sony's own tablet computer-television will stand a better chance in the marketplace.

Sony executives sincerely believe that they are betting on the right strategy and that the company will prevail in the digital era. They hark back to the fundamental core of the Sony spirit that Ibuka laid out in the founding prospectus in 1946: Innovation comes from the heart. Sony built a well-respected reputation over 50-some years by inventing great products, not by copycatting. That is what Sony executives call Sony DNA: the constant drive to dream and create.

The company may not always meet the standards it sets, but it tries. On its corporate website, the following statement, in technicolor, aptly sums up the soul and essence of what Sony strives to be: "We're not here to be logical. Or predictable. We are here to pursue infinite possibilities. We invite new thinking, so even more fantastic ideas can evolve… We take chances. We exceed expectations. We help dreamers dream."

NOTES

For further reading, see Peter Lewis, "Sony Re-dreams Its Future", *Fortune*, November 10, 2002, and Kuriko Miyake, "Sony showcases new VAIO line-up", *IDG News Service*, September 12, 2002.

Additional information in this chapter is taken from interviews with Masanobu Sakaguchi, Kei Sakaguchi, Jyunji Tsuyuki, Mack Araki, Kenichi Fukunaga and Eiichi Yamamoto, Sony employees in the U.S. and Japan.

INDEX